The Undercover Superhero

Mission Possible is an Inside Job

Anita Myers, CPC, CRCS

Book cover photo by Jonathan Roob of www.JohnathanPortraits.com

Publisher:

Rose Gold Publishing, LLC

www.rosegoldpublishingllc.com

ISBN-13: 978-1-7332638-3-2
ISBN-10: 1-7332638-3-7

Foreword

If you had to choose the playlist of music that best defined your life from childhood to now, what songs would you choose? What my dear friend Anita Myers has done is chosen hers. What she has done for you and I is to write the best book I've read on how one woman's experience can mirror our own. Maybe not the exact path, but certainly you will see your journey in hers. The value for us is that unlike any other author I've read before, she not only demonstrates the global challenge but specifically and step by step teaches what to do about it. In a world of vapid self-interest, Anita went through the painstaking and rare process of self-discovery, not for herself, but for the rest of us to benefit in our own journey.

From the 1st "fuck you" to the assholes that tried to break her to the ending sentence of calling you to reveal the undercover superhero in you to conquer the world, this book is filled with gems of wisdom!

Determine your role in relationships, optimize your opportunities, and then unleash your undercover hero! This is how the story starts and just picks up steam from there.

Anita captures full conversations from the 1st sentence through to the end with such clarity that you can identify red flags or green flags in your own relationships. Each and every example throughout her story is one I could identify with.

Thank you, Anita, for baring your heart and soul to the universe and to me and to the millions of readers who will find themselves in your words and reflections. Thank you for loving deep enough to bypass your pain for our relief. Relief from the belief that we are alone. We are not alone because of your unique decision to seek, analyze, accept, and teach.

Thank you,

Jason Sisneros - The Bald Avenger

Table of Contents:

The Undercover
Superhero

Mission Possible is an Inside Job

Anita Myers, CPC, CRCS

To the assholes who tried to break me:
fuck you.

I won.

Introduction
Playlist: Heal the Pain – George Michael

We like to think of America as Land of the Free, where everyone is loved and valued. But growing up as a child, I lived a different story.

I'm not the typical Indian, typical girl, typical teen, typical woman, wife, or mother. There's nothing typical about me. There was nothing typical about my parents either, but stereotypes, cultures, practices, habits and common experiences can make life one hell of a tsunami to surf through when you're a first generation American with parents who think, feel and act very differently from one another.

Juggling their two different cultures along with the melting-pot-perceived culture of the ever-changing American Way in the United States makes the idea of driving down the Autobahn blindfolded so much more doable.

What I saw in my childhood, my teen years, my young adult years and up to now has given me moments of absolute highs and tremendously low lows, and all of it has to do with how people interact with one another. When I dug a little deeper into the angsty "whyyyyyy!" that I'd feel over the different collections of SNAFUs and FUBARs I've kept in my lifetime's junk drawer, I noticed something. Underneath all the excuses used for people who misbehave there rested clear "cause stones" that were lodged in the minds of those who hurt people. The causes narrow down to:

- They were treated just as poorly, if not worse.

- They were misinformed, misguided and/or misled.

- They lived in lack physically and emotionally and learned what worked to survive.

And all of these main points unearthed a bigger recognition:

Emotional Wellness played a partial part or no part of their developmental equation.

Historically it seems that the culture of upbringing, especially outside of the United States, was much more focused on what I'd imagine to be an abuse of power. The default was set up with a master/servant and superior/subordinate mentality. Makes sense, then, to see the voracious desires among millions of people who set their minds to immigrate to the one country that gained a worldly reputation of being the Land of the Free.

There wasn't a whole lot of EQ spotlighted in history. Most books I've read taught more about inquisitions, take overs, and domination. That led to social structures akin to a caste system, class structure and the need to feel powerful in a dominant manner, with corporal punishment used as the tool. And parenting styles, work environment styles, and social functioning styles breathed that same air. Children of that time learned that way of life and even today, more grown-ups could probably say that they just dealt with their spankings, threats, bullying, and other negative experiences. It was the norm of their life. One might even believe that emotional wellness could classify as "sissy stuff" having been so desensitized to the actual positive value of emotional power.

It was a tougher scene for the children of today to imagine. A rougher emotional landscape to walk on. And while many today can say "hey, I got through it, so suck it up, buttercup," times are ever-changing.

Society is feeling the pains of being overwhelmed, tired, lost, depressed, and stressed. Bad habits are getting worse, limits are being ignored, boundaries are torn down, and the hardest outcome from these changes is that the quality of life is appearing to look dim at best in the hearts of too many wonderful and amazing people.

Entitlements have become the new flavor of attitudes we see on television and in our social circles, whether through social media or social gatherings. The ego is running past the point of no return in behavior where genuine gratitude is provided or received with an acronym and emoji through a selfie on a social media post.

Commonplace postures resemble heads facing downward, focused on the information being shared off of an electronic screen. And while I also love the networking and connecting benefits of social media, I can see the evolution of a disengaged, battered heart in the long run, where social phobias take place. While I encourage the benefits of technology and connecting with people globally, there is still a missing link that's valuable for the functioning and maintenance of a fulfilling life.

People need healthy, passionate, and positive relationships. And no, not just lovers. I'm talking relationships all across the board. Between singles, couples, spouses, managers to employees, neighbors to neighbors, parents to children, teachers to students, coaches to athletes, salespeople to prospects, humans to animals, you name it – there should be positive experiences by default between all parties involved. All of these connections hold massive potential to be fulfilling and fantastic through our ability to gauge our own emotional powers.

When I was a child, I recognized my level of passion and compassion, but was stifled and suppressed due to the agenda of other people's desires to control me. I wasn't someone who was taught to defend myself. I was taught to oblige and deal with it. Say nothing. Don't ask questions. Just do as you're told. The outcome had me following poor leadership, partnerships and connections. I saw a lack of a belief in love, worth and purpose so heavy that it led me to standing six feet from the edge of game over, until I made a decision that changed my whole world.

I don't want you to give up on love, in any form; not now, not ever.

Whether you know this or not, you are too powerful and incredible to settle or walk away from your purpose here on Earth. Even if you don't know what your purpose is, this is not the time to either settle, burn or destroy your life's canvas and lose your opportunities to grow – not when you're filled with powers that can fulfill you to the ends of the Earth and back.

It's time for you to explore and actually enjoy the journey you're given, while it's available to have it.

My intention in writing this book is three-fold:

- to help identify your values in relationships and your role in it

- to recognize how to avoid shortchanging your opportunities and experiences, and

- to take the 1st step in harnessing your mind power that will lead you to the beginning of mastering your Universe

Why?

Well for starters, there are superheroes and villains in our world. Villains became villains from dysfunctional, misguided people who either directly or indirectly taught them to do what they do. Superheroes arrive to redirect, rescue, and straighten that shit out to the best of their ability, all in the name of achieving peace, order, and harmony for the greater good.

But did you know there are more superheroes on deck?

These are incredible people living among us right now who hold great and mighty productive powers, but they're hidden in the shadows of doubt, insecurity, poor habits, incorrect definitions, false or misleading information that led them to stay exactly where they are, undercover in the shadows of someone else's greatness or control. These are our Undercover Superheroes.

You're an Undercover Superhero.

You are a magnificent, super-galactic superhero who arrived here masked as a human, struggling around trying to fit in the human society you were given. And of course, everything is cray cray in your world. Nothing's in order. We're shown chaos and calamity daily among humans. Criminals, criminal-ing all day long. Villains, villain-ing. Haters hating.

And not so much talk about lovers loving. Why? The human mind wants drama. So, if it's drama you want, it's drama you'll get. We live in what I'll call a WYWIWYG life by our own mechanism. If you read the acronym phonetically, it sounds more like Why We Wig (Wy-Wi-Wyg), as if to provide the question, "Why (do) we wig (out?)" and in the same acronym, the answer is actually contained within each letter's true meaning: What You Want Is What You Get.

Mentally, when we suffer from hard to adverse experiences, we desire quick and easy results, just so we can be freed from our negative feelings. Usually, these moments foster emotionally based actions with not a whole lot of logic allowed.

Remember that warning phrase, "Be careful what you wish for." We rush after what we think we want so much that we neglect what we actually need. Often, we don't even know or recognize what we need, being so busy in wanting-mode. We can even create our belief system based only on our wants and end up emotionally frustrated running in circles wondering how the hell to get out of it.

All relationships can feel from exciting to uneasy to scary when you're meeting someone either for the first time or after some time, after things between you two had gone sour before. In those moments we could feel vulnerable, annoyed, and fear the worst. We may even be guilty of prolonging a relationship that already ended emotionally, because of the way we feel. That's the power of emotion. Our emotions hold so much power that it can change our perspective of ourselves and of people and turn connections from zero to hero, and right back to zero if we wanted to.

Before embarking on any relationship of any kind, there are a few inner housekeeping procedures worth following.

Here's a quick, action-packed to-do list for you, to start:

- Roll your sleeves up and dig through the layers of hesitation within you to release your natural given powers.

- Bring balance between your state of mind, the power of your thoughts, actions, and reactions, and rebuild a belief system that supports those needs on an ongoing basis.

- Identify what love is and means to you, and why love would matter if you had it and if you didn't.

- Get your power back if you find yourself in an unhealthy, power-sucking toxic relationship – of any kind. Free yourself!

- Refuse the eclipses and shadows that cast doubt or negative feelings. Prefer to step out into your own light and reveal the Undercover Superhero within you.

I am an Undercover Superhero. Unapologetically.

Way over two decades ago, I didn't claim that name. I thought I may have been one, but I refused to feel it. There's a difference between the two. The former stays dormant in your mind and keeps you settled where you are. The latter makes you move to your next higher platform of living.

Undercover Superheroes live off the pulse of **worthiness**. They built their foundation around **respect**. And their actions are soaked in **commitment**. In this book, I'll share some personal stories that brought me to low points in my life, the actions taken, the powers uncovered, and the lessons and blessings that came from them. I'll introduce necessary powers, and more importantly, show you how to use them for the greater good. See, just because we all consider ourselves grown-ups doesn't necessarily mean that we're done growing. We keep growing and changing until our time comes to transition toward our next ethereal experience in pure energy form.

This is your time to get your real powers back. Reclaim ownership to yourself in a magnified way. Train to focus on important perspectives, actions, and reactions.

Get empowered emotionally, spiritually, and mentally to go from zero to hero in love, and in life. Once you've invested in building and reinforcing what really matters *to you,* these areas will deliver you to a new position in your life, and you'll uncover the superhero that's always been within you.

When you put the heart-work into what it really means to be who you are, you will never live the same way again. Your powers, once revealed, simply won't let you.

It's time to acknowledge the Undercover Superhero within you, and once you do, you'll never go back to the place you once lived. You'll move forward living a more creative, powerful clarity honoring the time and opportunity to seize your days instead of having your days seized from you.

Chapter One: My Love Story
Playlist: Going Under – Evanescence

Hi, it's really nice to meet you.
Wow, you're gorgeous.

I never met a woman like you before
you are genuine and beautiful.
Something amazing happens
when we are together.

I love how I feel when I'm with you.
I like your hair up, by the way. Looks real pretty.
Hi, Baby, why didn't you call me?
Just making sure you're okay.
I'm falling in love with you.

Wow, pretty dress, I like your hair up better.
I always want the best for you.
You know, I'm the only one who ever will.

I called you. Where were you?
Why didn't you answer?
You know, your "BFF" is just using you.
Stay away from her. Trust me.

Where was I? Out with the guys.
What is this, Twenty Questions?
You expect me to ask for your
permission next time?

Tell your mom you'll call her back.
You can talk to her when I'm not home.

You're wearing your hair up. Looks nice.
The shade of lipstick, though, what the hell is that?
Honestly, those colors are not flattering on you.
I upset you? Well, get over it.

I'll get you some nice things
that my girl should be wearing.
Stick with me, and you'll go far, baby.

I'm going to a party, but I can't take you with me.
It's just for me and my friends and their girlfriends.
I called you, and you never answered.
Don't ever do that again.

I do everything for you
and you thank me by being a selfish bitch.

Yeah, so the chair broke
I could have thrown it at you.
I can fix the chair, but you, no one can fix.

I know - I got out of hand. I'm sorry.
I get so upset because I care so much about you.
I love you.

You're going to pick your
stupid "girls' night out" over me?!
You're not being loyal.
I thought I told you to throw out that lipstick.

Give that to me. Look at your face now.
W-H-O-R-E. That's what you look like.

You think you're gonna find another man?
If I leave you, no one will want you.
Maybe I should let you go.

Stop crying. Get up. GET UP.
Jesus quit being a baby.
Stop fucking crying.
I'm sorry.

Honey, I didn't mean to hurt you.
I was afraid.
I thought I'd lose you.
I don't want to.

The girl was nobody.
Don't think too hard.
Your little mind
can't handle the pressure.

I swear on my mother's eyes,
nothing happened.
Would I say that if I were lying?
Go get your head checked.

Please don't leave me.
You're the greatest thing that
ever happened to me.
I can't imagine my life without you.
I can totally see you as my wife.

You're the bride I want to see
at the altar with me.
All I want is us. Forever.

You love me, right?
You love me.
Let's move in together
I think it's time.

Whose number is this?
Your doctor?
Bullshit.

Don't ever keep secrets.
Secrets are what bitches keep.
You're such an embarrassment.

Are you giving me shit right now?
Do you want to be alone for the rest of your life?
Don't fuck with me, you understand?
Don't act stupid.

You're crazy.
How many personalities do you have?
You're seriously Sybil.

You're blowing everything out of proportion.
You are such a pain in the ass.
You can't even take a joke.

You're not wearing that
you look like a slut.
Come here
I'll show you what
happens to sluts.

I'm sorry.
Omg, I'm so, so sorry.
I don't know what got into me.

Please don't cry.
I hate to see you crying
I'm crying.
I never cry.
But today I am.
I didn't mean to do that.

Please stop fucking crying!
I'm sorry, okay?
I'm sorry.

I love you.

According to the National Domestic Violence Hotline, 1 in 4 women aged 18 and older in the United States have been the victim of severe physical violence by an intimate partner in their lifetime. 1 in 3 raped. I'd have never imagined that I'd be a statistic in this arena, but I was. I called that dark poem A Love Story, with an obviously massive sarcastic tone to it.

Of course it wasn't a love story, but it was a story where the word "love" was abused. It was abused by way of constant manipulation and control. But this story of love as I saw it needed to happen; I would never have become the woman I am today if it didn't happen. This shitty poetic tale was all a part of the growth process within my spiritual chrysalis. This needed to happen so that I could eventually come to terms in redefining what love should feel like for *me*, instead of for others. I already knew what I was capable of doing and giving for anyone regarding love. I've never been apologetic for loving anyone; it was more about loving and respecting myself enough to have others loving and respecting me the same, or at least close enough.

I would think that I'd know better than to fall into the hands of a guy like the one in the poem. He was never my type at all and held no real manners. He did, however, hold the same deadly characteristics that I'd been trying to escape and free myself from: control, secrets, manipulation, narcissism. He groomed me into believing his worth was more valuable than mine.

He started off pouring words of care, desire and concern into me – the kind of words that filled spaces that were vacant for most of my life. He complimented me so much, he'd share how similar we both were in what we liked. He desired me. He wanted to know so much about me and showed such a fantastic passion for my welfare. He was persistent and was willing to talk to me all night. He'd call at any time to check on me to make sure I was ok, made me laugh, and did whatever he needed to do to show up, even when his life's schedule was demanding. He just made it happen. The sacrifices. The effort. The conversations. The care.

The way he held my heart, with intent to protect it – I went from never imagining I could ever be with a guy like him, to seeing him as the best choice in the market of single men out there. It felt like a spell, because beneath the emotional surface, the logical part of me questioned every acceptance of him that I made.

The emotional side of me loved everything about his effort, humor, and desire. The convincing factor was his confidence. I won't lie – I love anyone who knows what they want out of life, and when a man knows who he is and what he wants, and he chose you to be the woman who stands by him in his life? Big turn-on. If you ever saw the movie *Goodfellas*, the feelings were similar to the character Karen meeting Henry Hill, taking her through the restaurant, knowing everyone and everything, and she was his girl. I didn't know then, but I can say now, I was craving to be taken care of, because I was always on my own with very little to no support, encouragement, or sense of security. That father figure feeling felt fabulous, even within his massively fucked-up inner world.

I lived most of my life doing things out of fear and longing for acceptance. And this guy? He was simply mad about me; he loved me so much. Tears-in-his-eyes kind of love. Signing-the-Holy-Cross kind of love. "I-swear-on-my-mother's-eyes," kind of love. There was no one else in the world like me, and I'm the winning lottery ticket. I'd never seen such a strong force; he was going to love me forever, and where I was in my life, I thought being loved, desired and protected forever was a great picture painted. With all the control and frustrations experienced in my upbringing, and as independent as I ended up becoming, I secretly wanted to fall into a secure man's arms who knew I was the best treasure he'd ever had. I wanted a man to make sure I was okay. Someone who'd appreciate me for being a good woman. Someone who could be my oasis.

Looking back now, knowing all of his ugliness, I was living in so much lack that I was groomed to celebrate his low-level pros as it dominated over my high-level cons.

I was at an all-time emotional low point upon meeting him. My father yanked me out of college with only one more year left before graduating, because he "didn't feel like visiting" me (it's about a three-hour drive from Chicago to Peoria) and wanted me home.

Soon after, my first love from college had a paranoia that I'd leave him for another man once I moved. He suffered so much worry that he assumed the worst and cheated on me one drunk night with a gal he didn't even know. Self-fulfilling prophecy.

Immediately after that, my father bought a house in Atlanta, Georgia but never told my mom nor me about it. He just expected us to be happy, pack up, and move with him. His sole decision shocked me and my mom deeply. The shock pushed my mom into a terrible depression. And right after that, I gulped one of the hardest gulps in my life – I decided to defy my father's expectations of me in following them to Atlanta, and instead:

- scurried to figure out how I would remain in Chicago, attend college and handle life on my own,

- provided a presentation to him that he reviewed, red-marked and graded with a "C" and accepted his deal where he'd oblige his financial "duty" to afford for my education to graduate, as long as living, eating, and existing remains my responsibility, and

- decided to let my mother have my dog that was completely my responsibility to care for since he was a puppy. My mom and I grew to be so tight in our relationship, giving my dog would give her a part of me while she left with my father in a full-blown depression.

In short, life really sucked, then. I was left alone with my close friends away in college, continuing their life as usual. I took on multiple jobs within the week and night/weekend college classes to earn my degree. Through one of my jobs, I met the guy who introduced me to one of the unhealthiest, dysfunctional, abusive relationships I'd ever been in. I was his perfect target, and I never knew it.

I slowly became seduced into this guy's world of control. As confident as I thought I was, there was something about me that catered to his needs, and his needs, joined in with my ability to give, became a symbiotic, unwritten, unconscious agreement that I never logically would have accepted. It was a straight-up emotional ambush.

He came in like a kind, docile sheep. I just never noticed the wolf within. What really sucks about that analogy is that I actually love wolves, and I love sheep, but I hate wolves in sheep's clothing.

> Beware of false prophets, which come to you in sheep's clothing, but inwardly they are ravening wolves.
> Matthew 7:15 KJV

We don't always notice the intent behind the action of a predator like the guy I met. Think of an equivalence between the predator/prey and the narcissist/empath. Empathetic people like myself find peace in trust and openness; we empathetic hopeless romantics love it and prefer living off of those values. Narcissists know it and love that about us. We are the perfect match for narcissists – it's just that they're completely not the perfect match for us.

They do what they can to create and own strategies needed to become trustworthy and kind. They're the ones who match your needs and emotional pleasures well enough and have the set up for their trap practically down to a science. It's frighteningly similar to how serial criminals work, through trial and error, practice, and honing in on what the equation is so they can ultimately have what they want.

They find loopholes and hidden cracks in people's behaviors and conversations. They fill those cracks just enough to fulfill their agenda. It's the textbook narcissists way. But I wasn't an expert on narcissism then. The world he opened me up to was a world filled with lies, deceit, manipulation, and control.

All he needed me to do was get on board with his abuse cycle and I'd be destined to ride it forever. This kind of cycle is the kind that feels more like being caught in a rip current without a clue of how to get out of it. The travesty that comes from an ocean's rip current is that most people in it don't know how they got in it, or how to get out of it. They feverishly panic fighting through the impact of its force, wearing themselves out, settling, giving in, and drowning.

This type of jarring, nightmarish life-sucking experience that I and millions of people have experienced isn't only physically relatable, it's emotionally and mentally crippling, destroying, spiritually agonizing, depressing, and sadly not on anyone's radar to rescue at first sight, or second, or third, or ever.

With his desire and intent, I'd be forever caught and dragged as far away from myself as he could take me. He overwhelmed me with his intensity. I kept fighting and panicking, but from within. On the outside, I played the "I'm Good, Life's Great!" performance of my lifetime.

Emotional and psychological abuse is a beast.

All abuse is horrible, but intangible abuses like psychological, intellectual, and emotional are more unseen and undetected. Because of this, the severity of the attacks and destruction of one's emotional health quietly creates a domino effect that's nothing short of a great mental Rube Goldberg-type nightmare machine that reaches a horrible end. There are no celebrations for that kind of outcome. Well, except for the abuser.

Victims go through a systematic major mental and emotional loss of epic proportions. There's no MRI that can show the damaged battlefield in my heart that's left barely beating for my existence. And I wouldn't dare show that side of me, fearing how shamed and dismissed I would be by my family members. I was already ashamed of my choices, but like a spell, I had no idea how I fell so deep into the darkness of that abyss. The stricken, broken Titanic inside of me was sinking, while the outside of me was the band that kept on playing, "Nearer, My God, To Thee."

One thing I learned as a child was how awful it felt being shamed. I hated being shamed for every move I made. I was constantly compared to everyone else's success in anything, and then questioned why I couldn't be like them. According to all of them, someone else's child, spoke better, smiled nicer, laughed softer, had better hair, nails, discipline, grades…

argh – okay, ok, OK!!!

That was their focus; in every move I made and didn't make, it felt as if they had me striving to reach some kind of perfect that I never knew I'd never reach.

I repeatedly heard corrections, disappointments, and comparisons. I absorbed the sting of their words. I felt the hits and smacks, from the average slap across the face, head or body, to whatever striking tool my parents would find to administer the consequence. After a number of years, I could only feel like I came into this world so broken in the eyes of those who either created me or managed me in some way. Fixing me must have felt pretty much hopeless for them, so unless I figured out how to fix myself up enough to reach their standards, I felt that there was ultimately no real purpose for my existence. I was neglected, ignored, dismissed, or punished. It was either I change immediately, or I was going to be considered stupid, foolish, dumb, or useless.

And here I was in my 20s, in this emotional setup. I couldn't let anyone know that I was eyeballs deep in a dysfunctional relationship. One where a part of me thought it was absolutely horrible to be in, and the other part wondered if I'm just being difficult, because maybe this is how relationships really are? Maybe this is what it's all about?

By my upbringing and learned habit to do whatever it takes to avoid being shamed, it would've been a terrible idea at age 22 to ever let anyone think I was a sinking ship. I worked too hard to manage life on my own, go to school at night, and work multiple jobs a week to make ends meet. I fought hard for this! I proved through my mega presentation to my dad why I wasn't going to follow him back to Atlanta.

I had a plan.

I wanted to make a life in Chicago and bring my mom back to live with me. I wanted to let my toxic relationship with my father go with him to Atlanta.

I spent a year and a half trying to free myself from the cycle. Six escape attempts later, I finally did. I mean, yeah, it did leave me unconscious and bleeding out on my condo's floor before I gained that freedom from him – but hey, I was free.

How did this happen to me? How did I not get out of this sooner? And how in God's name, am I even able to talk about something so ugly and dark with anyone?

Let me take you back to my beginning, to give you the answers.

Chapter Two: My Genesis
Playlist: Daughters – John Mayer

My parents married in 1969. My father left everything he had and immigrated to the U.S. from India in 1970, and my mom followed a year later in '71.

My dad was from a tiny village in India. He left the country life and headed to the great, bustling city of Mumbai to move on up in his successful world. With focused eyes for success and importance, and as the eldest of three children, he simply and naturally wanted more. He wasn't an A-grade student – he was an A++++ kind of student with a brilliant mind that soaked up information easily. He gained a job in sales at a reputable appliance company in the city and met my mom there, who mesmerized him with her beautiful long hair, her style, and her evergreen class.

My mom was a very cosmopolitan woman who frequented get-togethers, attended many social functions and who also was a professional classical Indian dancer. She had hoped to travel to America with the dance company she was in while spending her time working as a secretary.

He was a salesman, and she, the secretary. Together they were the Indian version of the ol' American television show, *Green Acres.* I found that adorable. No arranged marriage here. He wanted her, he charmed her, and he got her.

I was born in Chicago, IL, in 1972. Nothing made my parents prouder than to have an "American child." Oh, my goodness, they were so glad to be in the United States. It was truly the Land of Opportunity for them. Even though they both were Indian, they wanted me to be American so badly that they named me an easy-to-pronounce name, and while each spoke a different dialect of the Indian language, they spoke to each other in the American English they knew, and preferred me to speak that way. They'd say, "You're American! You don't worry about speaking anything else." And life, with their little baby girl started out, as I heard, to be pretty good.

In the beginning.

My father's work had him working hard hours. His boss would keep him for 36 hours straight, leaving my mom (a fairly new bride and super new mom) alone in an apartment in the city. Being new and alone most of the time, she didn't know where to go, what to do and how to get around, when all she knew were the neighborhoods in India. They left everyone back home and were winging it in a new country. The frustration that typically comes with having a new baby probably didn't help either. She figured things out to not only accommodate herself but to accommodate me and my dad (and his ways).

Even though they both came from India, they came from two different regions, with different languages, different social settings, different cultural expectations and demands, different religious focuses, different food interests and preparations, different cultural attire – I mean, these two were completely different people in every way.

I guess in the end, looking back, these two had personalities and needs synonymous to oil meeting water – they just didn't mix, and they found out the hard way.

My childhood was similar to the life that many of my friends and acquaintances had who lived through the '60s, '70s, and '80s when it came to parental corporal punishment. It was part and parcel for parenting power. It went beyond the house, incorporating a collective beating via the neighborhood and community. They really played out the phrase, "It takes a village." I mean, aunts, uncles, neighbors, instructors, teachers, bosses (remember the Christmas classic *It's a Wonderful Life*? Poor George Bailey) and even nuns (fear The Penguin, Sister Mary Stigmata, of the movie, *The Blues Brothers*). I'm sure this kind of corporal punishment is still commonplace in traditional societies around the globe.

I remember the first sting on my hand from my dad when I was three that devastated my mom - because I was three. I still remember her telling me the "first time your father hit you," story. She'd grind her teeth in anger as she said it every time. I wasn't supposed to touch a drinking glass, but I did. I picked it up, and he thwacked my little hand really hard. "It's appalling. It's horrific. It's disgusting. He could have just said no. Or stop. Or taken the glass away. But no, he had to slap your tiny little delicate hand...." My mom was just beside herself that he would have ever laid a hand on me - that young. "You spank later. Not at 3!" she exclaimed as she reminisced. Well, at least she got my back for a couple of years.

After hands, belts, slippers, wooden spoons, wire hangers, strong finger flicks to the lip, and pinches to the arm, butt, waist, face or ear were administered for every possible wrongdoing in speaking (or lack thereof) and actions (or lack thereof), it was clear that corporal punishment was the way of the world for disciplinary action. If you ever saw Canadian comedian Russell Peter's *Comedy Now!* performance in 2004 that went viral, it went viral for a reason beyond being funny when you peek into the typical Indian household. It was relatable. As he says in the show, "...it doesn't matter where your parents are from, (if) they weren't born in this country, they will whoop your ass when you're growing up...." The Indian-accented phrase that echoed for the next decade among millions who saw the video is the looming threat of his father: "Somebody gonna get a hurt, real bad."

Corporal punishment, it is the thing to do to gain respect, based on major fear. It's the thing that had us kids say, "My parents are going to kick my ass..." or "My dad's gonna kill me." Or worse, we live in stress keeping secrets from them for the rest of our lives for fear of the d-word. Say it with me:

D-d-d...*Disappointment.*

This was the way; it might still be in many households, I suspect. But it's heavily frowned upon now since enough studies have shown that discussion and non-violent consequences can teach reason and logic-inspired reactions that can build strong, respectful people from the inside out. Violence, both physical and verbal, were no longer necessary to administer in order to achieve the parent's end goal. Smart, productive, and active listening-type of conversations became the better way for a healthier and satisfying relationship, developing good children who gain potential to develop into great adults in the long run.

Bullying and beatings were no longer required. Sucks that I wasn't a part of that breakthrough in parenting, but honestly, I wouldn't be the woman I am today, doing what I do today if things had gone differently.

To be fair, my words about my father and mother's parenting style aren't meant to demonize them. I share to address how important it is to recognize the possibility that the abuse in our life when we're older possibly stemmed from similar experiences and learned behaviors when we were younger. Abuses that may not have even been recognized as abuses that were administered as commonplace within our childhood with our parents, and supported by family members, relatives, community and or society or culture. To be able to see the power in the influence that controlling and dominating behavior gives and how that can impact who we are today by how we handle any conflict, with any person, in any setting.

Most of us, I'd imagine, have two personalities. No, I don't mean split personalities. I mean you behave one way when you are home, and another way once you step out into the world.

When I was out, my persona was about embracing the concept of being an American girl. No, not the doll. Just the average American kid who could be appreciated and accepted for being me, whatever that was. I followed trends. I wore the clothing styles of the American culture. But at home, I was not the same girl. I morphed back into the quiet Indian daughter who wouldn't dare showcase freedom. I followed their words as much as I could. Not because I respected them, but because I feared the beating. I never wanted to be slapped, in private or in front of guests. It's so humiliating and over things that I never thought were warranted a slap, a thud, or a pinch. My parents typically spanked first and then asked questions, or sometimes asked questions while spanking. I mean, shit, look at the dash in your life, they say. Well, look at these dashes. Imagine the dashes as a spank:

"Why – did – you – do – that – when – I – told – you – not – to!!"

The physical punishment only secured the emotional belittling, condescending, reverse psychology, do-as-I-say-not-as-I-do, master or servant mentality. And us kids? We simply toughed it out. Sounds a little badass, but the truth is, we survived it; it doesn't mean we healed from it. It just means we held it together on the outside while we might have been unknowingly still existing but broken on the inside. At this point, I bet some of my friends, and I can agree that we might as well be immortal having gotten through all the lashing, whipping, spanking, beating, hyperventilating cries and verbal abuse. We did get through it, but no doubt, many of us suffered. And often that kind of suffering carries on with us. The stress is almost like we're always in fight or flight mode, surviving another day.

With all our daily stresses of avoiding trouble, keeping our head above water, or disappointing controlling people, we've spent more time undergoing pressures that keep us in a constant state of anxiety and fear. Moments that lead us down the rabbit hole of depression and illnesses. Or maybe we project our frustrations upon others and develop bad habits consciously or unconsciously as a coping mechanism for ourselves.

For me, as a child, spanking and emotional abuse was the way of the world. When my father spoke, he was disgusted, apathetic, and belittling. He was always so much smarter than we were, and by the nature of his manners, it sure looked like he was proud of it. He was able to take one view that would seem exciting to others and crush it with his own intellectual perspective and criticism, paying no mind to the emotional makeup of that individual.

In public, he was a charmer. He had all the men leaning in to listen to his business advice, worldly thoughts, and guidelines to life. He also charmed the ladies with his wit and humor.

At home, it was a silent house, curtains closed, melancholy energy in the home as a general standard that was occasionally accessorized with arguments, fights, berating, belittling, and psychologically abusive control. And while I grew up in this scene, watching him tear my existence apart calmly through his crafted words and dismissive attitude; seeing him bring my mother from a confident and capable woman to a frail, under-loved, lost and fearful mother, I wondered what the whole point was in immigrating to the "Land of Freedom" if my mom and I couldn't really experience any freedom?

I had archived so many memories of those negative times, but because I had them where they were: deep in the mental vault to not look at again, I couldn't heal and overcome. I thought memories like that would be safer there, in that vault, but it wasn't in the long run.

Keeping tangled experiences, stones, and rocks that were thrown, and all the other verbal weaponry deep within me, only hurt me in different ways. It may be like an operating instrument or material left in the body of a person being operated. The patient might walk away assuming they're fine until the body reacts and says, "nope!" and rejects it. You're left in awful pain having no idea why, until you go check on that pain and realize what was left that didn't belong there. Once that's removed, your body feels relieved again, pain is gone, and you are physically and emotionally free. The focus is knowing that what was left there doesn't belong there anymore. Once you remove it, you're pain-free.

I'd have tears like a leaking faucet: forming slowly and dripping randomly when moments I wouldn't have imagined triggered me. Ever suddenly cry, and you have no idea why something so subtle had your heart break a bit or a lot? Look into what about the moment choked you up. What if that moment connected you to something in your childhood that needed attention and healing?

I knew over time, that if I kept ego-wrestling and avoiding the ugly memories, the needs, the cravings, the confusion, the sadness – I'd never heal from it. It would only eventually transform into something else because this kind of energy doesn't do well staying dormant. It has to finish its journey.

And if experiences that created those memories are left unresolved, with lessons unlearned, it's my belief that it will be replayed in as many different circumstances as needed. The repeats take place in order for us to do the work within ourselves. To, how I'll describe as, "completing the incomplete sentence." The unfulfilled experiences and the unfinished businesses in our emotional lives are like reading incomplete sentences. Once we can complete the sentence, we can work with the bigger messages that we couldn't see before. Decisions become easier to make, and feelings are freed from burden.

Memory is an amazing power that we're so fortunate to have and is gifted to us for our survival and development. The ability to recall anything is actually an amazing gift to us that's often gone undetected and/or underrated. When we look at memories of negative experiences, we might tend to naturally default to a negative reaction like:

- We neglect. We focus on other things and stop paying attention to it, forget about it, and it remains right where it is.

- We avoid. We simply shut down, change subject and don't go there. We just don't want to talk about it. Ever.

- We sweep it under the rug. Where we've swept other things to look at and deal with later. Much, much later.

We negatively react. Naturally, negative memories influence us to feel hurt, depressed, confused, angry, or a combination of them. The ugly experiences can negatively charge ourselves to either

- develop false definitions based from negative experiences and incorrect assumptions

- act in revenge against someone who's hurt us (some of the best action-packed movies are built around that topic, btw)

- sabotage self-improvement and healing by way of adopting poor coping mechanisms (i.e., taking on bad habits, self-inflicting damage, suicide, etc.), and/or

In summary, engaging in negative reactions from negative experiences can slow down or even halt the process in overcoming and growing through the problems we're given.

The alternative is engaging in positive reactions from negative experiences. I know what you're thinking: "Yeah, Anita – when something's negative, you want me to jump for joy?? Not gonna happen." I agree with you; that's usually not going to happen. What I'm suggesting you do is review what happened, recognize your reaction, and train your reaction to cope better. If you typically lose your temper, get depressed, complain, whine, yell, and stress out, it's not a horrible thing; it's who you are, and it's a normal reaction – but if you want to react better to these happenings, I'm promising you that your stress level, blood pressure, overall clarity, and perspective will improve and allow you the space to do better, recover and move forward.

How? Feel. Give the moment the attention it needs. Find the time and feel the feeling. We don't avoid the feelings of falling in love, getting an amazing gift, or other positive moments. Why can't the negative moments get the same respect that they need to process? Feel the feeling of loss, disappointment, frustration, whatever that feeling is if something negative happened. Your most favorite rock concert canceled at the last minute? Your car broke down on the highway? Laundry machine broke mid-cycle? A friend betrayed you? Feel the moment. Grieve. Feel angry. Feel it for five to ten minutes. Yes, it IS shitty. It does suck. It's awful. Just feel the moment and give it a short amount of your time, and then work your way to heal from it immediately after.

Just think – your body naturally does this with no direction or training: when your stomach's upset, your body has you running to the bathroom and lets it all out. You can't keep it in as much as you try to control it. Your body won't let you. And when it's all over, you're on the couch or in a bed, resting up until you're better. You'll wonder what the hell happened. And you're going to think and talk about it till you know the answer. And you'll probably make decisions to avoid that from ever happening again if you can help it. And then, that's it. You're healed, and you go back to life as normal, having only the memory of how that royally sucked.

Your body rejects and ejects negative experiences. It rids the crap, pauses, and recovers so it can move forward and live for you. Here's how you can reciprocate:

There are six positive reactions to help recover from negative situations that can help you to rid the crap, pause and recover. Just think WOBBLI – like if your mind feels wobbly over a negative experience or circumstance:

1.   **W**ho's driving?

There are two people in a car: Logic and Emotion.

Imagine Logic as a mom or dad, and Emotion as a two-year-old toddler, fully submerged in the "terrible twos" stage, frustrated and wanting attention. One is driving, and the other's buckled in a five-point-harness car seat in the back. Who's driving? Your natural answer is, "The parent is driving." In a real-life scenario this is the answer anyone with common sense would respond. But when we're talking about Logic and Emotion in a time of frustration, anger, confusion, it seems that Emotion (a.k.a. the toddler) is the driver, and Logic (the parent) is in the car seat in the back.

According to a study from AAA Foundation Research says, "approximately eight million U.S. drivers engaged in extreme examples of road rage, including purposefully ramming another vehicle or getting out of the car to confront another driver...."

In the United States, the age of drivers starts out between 16 – 18 years old, depending on the state. And most road-ragers, tail-gaters and confronters, I'm guessing, could be between the ages of 20 – 65. My point is, as much as you'd like to imagine logic being the driver of that car, it's primarily Emotion that rules the driving.

Can you imagine a child going through the terrible twos and driving? What would you suppose would happen?

"It's completely normal for drivers to experience anger behind the wheel, but we must not let our emotions lead to destructive choices, said Jake

Nelson, AAA's Director of Traffic Safety Advocacy and Research.

"…emotions lead to destructive choices."

When a negative situation occurs, lead with logic. Keep emotion in the car seat and wait until you get home to help your (inner) kiddo out.

(Source: https://newsroom.aaa.com/2016/07/nearly-80-percent-of-drivers-express-significant-anger-aggression-or-road-rage/)

2. **O**ptions

You have options in how you can handle the moment. Positive, productive options are like the mental protein that helps us reach for success. When upsetting things happen, I've learned to allow myself the time to mourn, frustrate and feel angry that XYZ happened, but then I choose to "flap my wings" with the remaining four options below to recover and rebuild if needed. Eckhart Tolle shared a memorable story in *A New Earth: Awakening to Your Life's Purpose*, about the behavior of two ducks after a fight (a negative experience): "[After] two ducks get into a fight, which never lasts long, they will separate and float off in opposite directions. Then each duck will flap its wings vigorously a few times, thus releasing the surplus energy that built up during the fight. After they flap their wings, they float on peacefully, as if nothing had ever happened.

If the duck had a human mind, it would keep the fight alive by story-making. This would probably be the duck's story: 'He thinks he owns this pond. He has no consideration for my private space...' As far as the body is concerned, the fight is still continuing, and the energy it generates in response to all those thoughts is emotion.

Your options are to either hold on to the story or let go so you can permit love's energy to fill you back up. Between the two, go for the latter. Then flap your wings.

3.   **B**reathe – Think about all the times breathing is spotlighted:

- when a woman is having labor contractions to ease the pain.

- when a baby's born, the cry that tells us air has reached the itty-bitty lungs and is ready for the world.

- when someone hyperventilates in a crying or anxiety spell to calm inner emotional chaos.

- when someone wants to hit a very complex target with weaponry (bow/arrow, rifle, etc.) to command stillness.

- when someone steps away, sits alone, meditates, sleeps, to bring clarity to the mind.

When negative experiences take place, we engage in shallow breathing. Shallow breathing and stress work in the following cycle: stress causes shallow breathing, and shallow breathing stresses us out. This turns into chronic stress that we live with, which lowers the production of Natural Killer cells and other immune cells that develop to protect our body from illnesses. The purpose of our breath is to not only be alive and stay alive, but to live well.

We're given an average of 16 breaths a minute which, if we lived to 80 averages to about 672,768,000 breaths. So, what will you be doing with your life in those breaths? How fulfilling will those breaths be? What is worth spending your breath on? What words, what kind of delivery, what screams, cries, vents, lectures, and monologues will be riding off the waves of your breath? Make your breath relevant from within by investing in how you breathe, and what you use your breath for – don't use your breath to occupy someone else's auditory real estate, if they're not buying. Let your breath live well for you by giving it the attention it needs from you. You have a symbiotic relationship with one of the greatest powers in your existence, and you probably don't even know it. But now you do, and you can do something really good with it.

Source: https://medium.com/thrive-global/breathe-5749aeb9f4f0

4. **B**lessings

Negative experiences can often have blessings hidden within the conflict. Whether the event has you growing wiser for your future actions or by learning something new, in most cases you'll find blessings hidden within the conflicts. Look for them. Blessings are gifts that add more power to your ever-growing power supply.

Finding these blessings will eventually train your perspective into looking for them more than dwelling in the ugly of a moment that became history. The blessings end up revealing things to be grateful about, and the teachings will eventually transform you.

5. **L**essons

In every experience, you have either lessons or blessings. You could also be fortunate enough to find a lesson within the blessing or a blessing within the lesson. That gives you a fantastic divine buy-one-get-one. Come on, ya can't beat that!

In difficult experiences, shift your thinking from melancholy to curiosity, fear to adventure and find what the lessons you needed to learn were supposed to be. I tend to default to that perspective shift with everything that frustrates me, which takes me from frustration to inspiration.

There's a book I read to my daughter that shares Zen stories. In that collection is a parable of two monks and a woman: "Two monks were traveling from one monastery to another. They were celibate monks, even not allowed a direct gaze at women.

After a long walk, they came to a river, which they had to cross. The river was flooded, and there was no way that they would get across without getting wet.

One lady was also at the banks of the river, wanting to cross. Monks decided to cross the river by walking through the shallow part of the river since the lady also needed to get on the other bank, one of the monks without much ado, carried her on his shoulders, and soon they reached the other bank, where he set her down.

The lady went her way, and the two monks continued their walk in silence. The other monk was really upset, finding the other monk's act disturbing…

After some time, the confused monk couldn't stand the thought and asked the other monk, "We are not allowed to look at other women, not touch them. But you carried a woman across the river?!" The other monk had a smile on his lips when he replied, "I put her down when I crossed the river, are you still carrying her?!"

Use your mind to learn more in your moments than to lose the meaning that it was meant to give you.

Source:https://spiritual-minds.com/stories/zen.htm

6.   Intent

When someone hurts you, it's usually because that person was hurt, either by you or someone else in their life. If you were the source of their hurt, however, you can settle your mind through doing the work to taking accountability and proper measures so you can offer a genuine apology to the action that hurt them, allowing them the space to heal.

If you weren't the source of their hurt at all, and they hurt you, you can do the work to forgive them knowing that they're suffering in some way and took it out on you.

There's one reminder that now appears as my default mantra when moments of ugliness arrive, where people insult, hurt, or do something to be rude or disrespectful toward me, and it wasn't warranted: Happy people don't do unhappy things or behave in unhappy ways toward others.

If you really think about it, happy people are just that – happy. They forgive. They let go. They don't really care about the little issues. They can translate what someone really means and find most situations passable for emotional consumption. Even when someone wrongs them, happy people react with more understanding behind the circumstances, and offer consequences that make way more sense than aggressive fire and brimstone persuasion to teach you a lesson.

Happy people heal and forgive because they're happy. Most people who have you jumping over hoops, and still find fault in your jump and landing, are suffering somewhere inside within their own emotional history, probably protecting the pain as they push along life's bitters. Their pain isn't for you to heal, it's for them to heal – but it's open season for you to forgive them because they aren't at the same conscious level to do the work and heal themselves as you might be.

Your better action is to forgive, for your peace of mind, and pray for theirs. When you can notice that, you might not let the moment affect you as much as you'd imagine.

Lastly, if they had no intent in hurting you, you can do the work to learn what caused you to feel the way you do, and heal what hurt you.

Sometimes we get triggered by something someone said, who never intended to hurt us. Sometimes we paint things with broad brushstrokes to protect ourselves. We might even hold high expectations in the people around us because we never want to be hurt by anyone again. We can train ourselves to diminish the size of the brush and release opportunities to heal. We might then discover the good behind the people who we're speaking to.

The intent is a crucial factor to put into your thoughts when people seem to create negative experiences in your life. It's the one area that, once I'm aware of the presence of intent, I can handle it appropriately, and keep my inner toddler buckled in the backseat.

Chapter Three: My Personal Identity Theft
Playlist: Just A Girl – No Doubt

When I was a kid, I really struggled with my identity in terms of who I was according to them, vs. who I believed I could be, according to me. When it came to my identity, the struggle was two-fold:

1. being born in the United States with parents who immigrated from India, and

2. being a child to two totally different types of people from two very different parts of India.

The combination of my mom's cultural and religious traditions, her interests in fitting in within the culture of America, along with my father's cultural, religious traditions, and his interests in fitting in within the new country; her way of parenting and his way of parenting, and America's ever-changing, ever-trending and always evolving "American Way" that captured the hearts of people all over the globe were the basic ingredients that contributed to my pretty decently dysfunctional tiny family within our melting pot of a nation.

To be an American girl and yet honor the Indian culture is no walk in the park. I suspect my parents also felt the pressures of fitting in after leaving their families and settling in a completely different environment, language, religious concentration, culture, and food.

My dad was a South Indian vegetarian who always joked with me about the chicken who walked around with one leg because I was eating a fried chicken drumstick my mom brought from Kentucky Fried Chicken. Through his teasing, though, I could see his compassion for animals. That's one thing I recall about my father that still touches my heart.

He had a love for animals in a way that was actually beautiful. He saw no reason why we should keep cats and dogs in the house. Or a bird in a cage. Or a fish in an aquarium. He felt that they should all be free to enjoy their world and not control them in ours; he felt sorry that any animal was in the house when he believed they deserved to enjoy the outdoors. He understood the domesticated animal, but deeper in his heart I know he'd want to see them set free.

I think if he were alive, he'd rather prefer to go on a safari and take joy seeing animals in their natural habitat, than visiting a zoo where they're "locked up behind bars and confined" as he'd tell me with disgust in his tone. As a kid, he saw his mom scaling, gutting, and cutting the head off a fish when he was younger, and it immediately changed him. No interest in any meat. Ever. Remained a vegetarian from then on.

And my mom? She was from the booming state of Maharashtra and city of Mumbai, India. She's a cosmopolitan woman in a busy world. She loved family, parties and gatherings, and was very social. She admired the class and grace of old Hollywood actress Sophia Loren and First Lady Jacqueline Kennedy Onassis.

In her life, there was always something going on in the city, and with her being a professional dancer and a secretary in a pretty big company, she was feeling good with her life. She was a non-vegetarian who loved great food. She spoke French, English and several dialects of the Indian language, and loved having conversations, discovering what good was tucked in their hearts along the way. She had compassion for animals, yes, but had a massive compassion for people.

When I think of a scene that can best show the difference between my parents, it's from this one time in Chicago where we passed by a homeless person. My mom gave him a leftover plate of food, and my dad reacted very similar to how the character Archie Bunker of, *All in The Family*, would react toward his wife Edith, mumbling "aw geesus" and gesturing a one-handed swipe over his face to calm himself down. He'd whine, "Why are you giving that man anything? He's homeless! That's who he is. Let G-d deal with it. That's not our issue!" And try to drag her away as she's trying to befriend and hear the backstory of the homeless man.

He still had remnants of the caste-system mentality swirling in his blood. Who you were born as in the social structure is who you'll remain to be. Interestingly, he was a contradiction in his own belief system. He came from a poor background and made a decision to leave his village to become something more significant than what he knew he could never be if he stayed where he was. And as he rose to the top of his game in career and finance, he still viewed hired help as just that – hired help. He'd leave food out for a cat or dog and enjoy learning their behavior and was fascinated over them.

And my mom? Screw the cat or dog, feed the human!

When I think more in-depth about both of their behaviors of that one example, I saw a woman who saw people who were misunderstood, made mistakes, didn't have love to help them through, and thought that maybe a conversation could help them change their feelings from despair into hope; animals don't have a choice, so they'll manage however they will manage.

My father came from very poor beginnings. He cannot fathom anyone who would prefer life on the streets over life in a beautiful home that they earned. To him, that was the most fulfilling feeling: honor your duties and work hard, and that reaps the reward. Not lying around asking for handouts. Not when your brain and body functions properly. Get up! Or stay down and remain stupid.

His logic was always spot on with everything I heard in terms of education, which I found admirable and desirable. I wanted to know as much as he did. And my mom's love for life, compassion, and respect for people was something I loved so much. But as their only child, being trained by them? Ugh. That was kind of a fucking disaster.

They were like oil and water. If they didn't fight, they bickered. If they didn't bicker, it was silent. And their rules in parenting were mostly not the same. She hated how he confined and controlled me, and he hated how she wanted me to have freedom and independence. And I? Honestly, I just wanted their noise to stop.

I wanted to see them in love as I saw in the shows I watched. Why couldn't they be like Mike and Carol Brady of '70s television series *The Brady Bunch*? They worked so well together, and they dealt with six kids! I was only one!!! But my parents had their own cultural, and religious differences. Differences in just about everything, and this parenting lab with a pair of immigrants with a 1st gen American was cracking at the seams.

I learned the term "dysfunctional" later in my life. It felt like the perfect word for the way life felt at home. I couldn't please either of them, and according to the way they worked, my job was to please them by accomplishing what they expected of me. And it was a figure-it-out/cause-and-effect/trial-and-error set up to never meeting their expectations.

Guidance on how to do anything was usually met with a high level of disappointment accessorized with heavy eyerolls and sighs, grinding teeth and foul language under their breath, and spankings/beatings, because I didn't do it as they imagined.

I hated learning math and despised learning from my father because of his quick strikes to my hands, legs or head when I didn't recite the multiplication's table properly or answered a trick question correctly. Questions were interrogations and woe be to your soul if you got the answer wrong.

As I write this, let me make something clear here about the physical spanks and beatings: I didn't go through some massive horrific, practically fatal physical abuse. Yes, they hit me. Often. Yes, wooden spoons were broken over me. Belts and hangers welted me, flip-flop-marks on my shoulders and back, whatever. Yes. That happened for most of my childhood. But if I could focus on what I feel was worse than that, it was the heavy, hard-hitting emotional abuse that systematically happened every day to me, my mom, and us as a pair. Add in the support for such ugliness when family members or friends either nod their head to agree, or laugh, or contribute. And the community that has people in positions of some kind of authority who do the same and are supported to behave in this way. I'm sharing this knowing so many kids who are now adults got the crap beaten from their parents, and while they survived that ass-whoopin', and even forgive it, just like I do, their personality might still bury pain from a broken, ripped, shredded and neglected heart because of the emotional abuse that most likely accompanied the experiences.

It wasn't long before I became visually and energetically sensitive to words, delivery of words, body language and behavior. I developed an ability to see and feel disappointment, boredom, disconnection, the beginnings of anger and disgust fairly quickly in someone.

Kids never want to be a burden to their parents, but when parents act out their anger, frustrations and, knowingly or not, take it out verbally/physically on their kids, pan life's camera to the heart and mind of the kiddos – it holds great potential to cut deep, even if they don't show it. The physical punishments hurt, yes, but the consistent emotional annihilation of character and hope feel like a slow torture towards imminent death to positive energy and self-worth.

On the receiving end, receiving mixed signals of being a good girl or a bad daughter spun my emotional structure into a dilapidated home hit by an EF5-rated tornado. Between my parents, he always defied and undermined anything she wanted to see happen for me, and because she stood up for herself, she was pegged an arguer. Full double-standard home, do as I say, not as I do. If she questions, she's a fighter. If he questions, he regards himself intelligent. If she said, "go," he'd say, "nope."

I remember when she found a strapless, solid black velvet dress for me to wear for my high school senior Homecoming dance that she felt was beautiful and classy. He saw it, and when she asked him what he thought, he bent his opened newspaper inward, and looked over his bifocals at me, then flipped the newspaper back to his reading saying, "She looks like a call girl." (I forced myself to take that as a compliment. Sometimes when you know truth from fiction, translating what he said to what I preferred to hear helped. I mean, look - he could have said I look like an ugly monster. Call girl wins.)

Going through their tug of war being their rope was horrible and, honestly, pleasing any of their wishes as a kid was near to impossible because they were stuck in a tumultuous relationship of their own and within themselves.

I was their dot in the very first video game "Pong" when it came to my identity. There were two distinct messages directed at me:

- Be a good Indian daughter, not a vagabond American girl.

- You're American! Be proud of that. You're not some Indian servant!

AGH. Was I their Indian daughter? Should I be their American daughter? Am I an American? Or Indian? Over the years, through a lot of quiet crying, soul searching and frustrating, I decided that no matter what anyone said, I was going to be what I believed reflected the real American Indian: Born in America, with whatever flecks of Indian cultural blood that pumped within my veins.

And that was that.

Chapter Four: My Childhood
Playlist: Oh Father – Madonna

I watched a video on social media a couple of years ago that showed a husband, wife, and their baby. The wife's holding their baby. The husband, who's lovingly smiling at his baby, has a full beard. He's making his baby laugh, and all sorts of love is exchanged. The husband then heads to the bathroom and after a little while returns back to his baby, but now beardless, clean-shaven, smooth as a baby's bottom. He says hello to his baby and tries to welcome the little one as he did before, but his baby doesn't recognize him. His new look scares the baby who begins to bawl, and bawl hard.

For entertainment purposes, so many adults and parents find this kind of experience to watch so adorable and cute, probably presuming that the baby will get over it once it realizes that he's just silly ol' daddy – but I didn't see the video that way. I saw a baby pause in shock, and then bawl in discovering a message of, "daddy is gone." Of course, we as viewers knew daddy was still there, but psychologically these pranks work to only entertain the grown-up, not the young baby whose brain is only beginning to develop comprehension.

Naturally, children are supposed to connect and attach to appearances. They're dependent upon that, as well as the energy of the parent and the scent that comforts them. The brain of a baby is in its early stage of development so the child can't presume what adult's brain can. The sudden change in appearances become something close to a temporary nightmare for the little one. Why?

Visual abandonment.

As soon as we attach ourselves with security, to throw in the feeling of abandonment becomes a direct shot to the heart, annihilating its comfort zone. The emotional core is obstructed. Children aren't prepared and don't develop well while in the discomfort zone. I mean, just think about it, even within most of the animal kingdom, baby animals get a designated time frame for developing and training with their parent(s), then they're weaned off and on their own. So while this little video engaged in a temporary shock and stunt between parent and child, if we pay attention we see toward the end that the feeling of funny-ha-ha for them turns into a slight feeling of oh-crap-regret for daddy and mommy while he tries to calm and hopefully reestablish his fatherly status with the little tear-soaked cutie pie who never saw that coming.

It's a reminder to us of the significant importance in the need for connection, comfort, and dependency that builds the emotional core kids need from their parents – one where parents benefit in the long run from focusing on providing until their kiddo(s) are ready to conquer the independent world that's waiting for them.

Why did I bring this up?

Because I had a relatable nightmare, but it didn't involve beards and shavings. It did involve happily busting the door open into my parents' bedroom to surprise and welcome my father back home from his overseas trip. It involved feeling the backdraft flash in front of me, revealing my father, a pair of wine-filled glasses, and a woman who didn't resemble my mom at all.

Wait - wasn't mom in New York visiting a girlfriend to take a break from all the fighting and embarrassment over a rumor in our neighborhood? The explosion of all thoughts and reasons consumed me as I watched him leap off the bed and slam the door right in my face.

"Holy shit."

That was the first time I ever swore out loud. I remember the first time I ever uttered anything close to a swear...

"Mom? What does effyuceekay mean?" I thought what I heard kids chanting about at school recess was one whole foreign word that was code for something. Boy, did I get that wrong. Hearing that, in a split second she stopped what she was working on over the stove and whacked me so hard across my face, I lost all balance and fell down a few stairs. I was flat on the floor at the bottom and saw my mom's head lean over as my eyes focused back from the shock of the slap-and-fall moment. "You ok???" She yelled, half pissed to high hell that I ever attempted to speak that word, and half-hoping I was still alive. "Yeah..." I responded. I imagined she'd say, "Omg, honey I'm so sorry!!" while running down the three steps toward me to hold me in her arms.

"Good. Get up, and don't *ever* say that again!!!" she exclaimed and went back to stirring some curry on the stove. That curry, I thought. It was like the better sibling. She tended to all the food more than me and I hated it. Fuck that curry. It got more attention than me. Fuck you, curry. Just fuck you.

I grabbed my heart with both of my hands and froze looking at that closed door. I was beyond stunned. I covered my face with my hands. I found myself repeating the words and getting louder, under my covered face. "Holy shit. HOLY SHIT!!" I felt like my brain was going to explode. I began to sob.

"How could you do this to mom..." I felt so overwhelmed in pain, anger, and shock. I kept sobbing, face-in-hands as I walked away from the closed door, down the hall to the living room couch. I fell into my mom's best friend's arms who was watching me at her house while my parents were gone and had seen everything.

It was Friday. I asked her to take me to my house early to decorate the walls before he returned with a homemade "Welcome Home, I love you!" sign. He was supposed to return on Sunday.

"Fucking liar!" I yelled as I bawled through my auntie's sweater as she was holding me. I didn't care if anyone heard me swear then. I was scared, confused, heart-shattered and in my mind, insanely furious. I kept thinking, they're still in there, in that bedroom. He never ran out to console me and explain. The door was still shut.

As a kid I wished I had the powers to shoot laser fire out of my eyes and burn my dad and that woman to the ground. Who the hell is *she*? A part of me felt like screaming "This is my mom's house! and her bed! and no one messes with my mom!! **Especially if you're messing around with my dad??!!!** The thoughts in my mind were full of rage and disgust. That piece of shit, whore. I should break away from the hug I was in, and go in that fucking room, and kill the bitch. So much for being a good girl.

My tears left me after a while, and I sat up quietly, wiping my tear-and-snot-drenched face with the long sleeves of my top. I heard a rustle. The bedroom door opened.

I saw a Caucasian woman walk out of the room with her head down. I know this because my eyes were glued hard on every single move from that doorway. I wanted her to look in my eyes and die from regret instantly right in front of me. But she wouldn't look at me. She kept her head down and went toward a fur coat, picked it up, wore it –

Omg. That fur coat.

When I walked in through the front door, I saw that fur coat resting on the end of our sectional. *I thought that coat was a gift my father bought my mom from his overseas trip. That fur coat was HERS??*

ASSHOLE!!!!!!!!! To think he actually bought my mom a fur, and to realize he's been cheating on her and that fur was the other woman's coat – enraged me. Did he even go on that trip? Was he with her all this time?? She picked up the fur coat, wore it, and with her head still lowered, whispered, "I'm sorry..." and walked out.

How long was this going on? When did this start? And why that woman?? *Who the fuck is she?* I hated being a well-behaved girl. My emotions wanted to fly out of the front door of my house, leap onto that woman and peel the skin off her face with my nails and listen to her scream until she died. I wanted to protect my mom, my home, my heart. I wanted to kick my father out and watch G-d take him from me and my mom forever.

My brain was ready to split into a billion pieces. I wanted to have instant jet engines and wings appear and fly me to wherever my mom was in New York and tell her everything, immediately...

Mom, we've been betrayed. He abandoned us. He never loved us. You didn't need him anyway. You deserve better. So do I. Hop on my back, and I'll fly us to Hawaii. We'll find a new husband for you who'll be a great dad to me, and we will live happily ever after. Come on, Mom. You and me.

I had a plan.

But instead, reality had me watch a woman who was in my parents' bedroom with my father walk out with that fur and close the door behind her.

I used to think furs were so classy and fantastic at the age of six, seeing the rich and famous wear them in the '70s. I was nine when this happened. That idea of fur? Dead, just like the animal killed for it.
After the door closed, the home I lived in now fell into an uncomfortable silence. Nothing was said. I could only hear myself breathing and felt my heartbeat practically out of my chest. I became instantly depressed. The man who I thought was my hero, who knew everything under the sun, did everything right, said everything correctly, who had all these unachievable expectations of me and had beat me and belittled me as much as he could to understand those expectations, that man royally betrayed my mom and me that day.

While he never actually left us, that was the starting day of his emotional abandonment toward me.

And I believe I ran away from home in my mind. Abandonment doesn't have only to take place in the physical sense. Think about this for a minute: what's worse to you – having someone no longer want to be in your life and leave you, or having someone no longer want to be in your life and stay, fully and reluctantly invested but not out of love, but out of duty. Reminding you daily that you're a burden, a liability, and just not important enough to the overall parent agenda? That others meant more to him than you? As the receiver of the latter, I can say I'd have rather seen him leave.

I'm sure mom and I would have struggled, but we'd have eventually figured it out. Him staying and infusing an I'd-rather-not-be-here energy in the house, his knowing that his wife and child are secretly painful, annoying burdens, and finds fault with everything we say or do – it would only become seismic emotional injustice that later culminates into physical illness, depression, anxiety and just an all-around loss of self-worth. I know this because that's what happened.

He painted this picture of himself to me that had me see him as a strong leader who knew everything. That day, he revealed a completely different person to me. He became someone who couldn't be trusted. When I reminisce about the happiness I had in attempting to surprise my dad while busting the door open, I still can feel that emotional backdraft explosion followed by the sheer shock, despair, and abandonment combo deal I received as he slammed that door in my face.

He came out of his bedroom. I didn't want to look into his eyes. I just saw his blurred image, which was enough. He sat in the chair that was facing the couch I was sitting on with my mom's best friend. I didn't want to look at him anymore. My mind was only occupied with my mom's face. I shut down. I no longer had the interest to know why anything happened. I didn't even know about sex yet to even comprehend what happened in that room, and my inner anger was off the charts. I'm surprised I didn't just drop dead right there with the intensity of everything I felt, but I guess I wasn't supposed to die yet.

He started talking to my mom's best friend, breaking the silence with an uncomfortable giggle. Hearing that giggle, however uncomfortable it was, made me want to lunge at him and take him out. I didn't want to hear to his voice, let alone find any of this funny while my eyes were swollen and chest hyperventilating from crying.

Ugliness crawled out of his mouth. Secrets, lies, and deceit was all I was consumed with. And based on his body language, he grandstanded the world's largest ego I think I'd ever known to mankind. I heard justifications and excuses from him. That what I saw I didn't see. What it was, wasn't. I heard laughter at how silly all of this was. How foolish I was to even consider such a farce. I heard enough. I didn't care about his words anymore. I just wanted to know when he'd leave my mom, so I could take care of her and find her a better man. I had zero reasons or room for forgiveness. It wasn't going to happen that day.

He turned his attention to me. "So, can you understand that what you saw was not at all what you saw. She was wearing light, faded jeans, she wasn't naked, honey..." he said.

I think I killed him a thousand times in my mind. And I hated that I still loved him because he's my dad. How do people do that so easily? Just buy into the lie so quickly and condescend to the person who literally just busted them? How do interrogation officers handle that when they know the criminals committed the crime and they lie so unbelievably well? I was floored that he had the nerve to manipulate me to believe him. I saw what I saw, and I called bullshit.

"Oh? Oh yeah. I guess so. Maybe I got it wrong..." I responded. Of course, I wasn't wrong. I was just calling his bluff. I tried to actually buy into the ugliest words I'd heard coming out from his mouth. I can't describe the feelings darting through my mind. I had power enough to fight him with what I knew because I knew they were true, but I was slightly chained down by my nine-year-old heart because I still wanted his love and approval of me. As messed up as it was, as his little daughter, I was willing to play the part long enough to buy into his delusional lie. Until I could be old enough to get the hell out of there and take my mom with me.

I think it's incredibly ignorant for parents to assume that kids know nothing. I think every adult I've ever asked agreed that as their parents looked at them while they were having adult conversations, they played the I-dunno-anything card when they were kids. We all acted like we were still playing with our toys, still sleeping, or we just gave our parents what they wanted to hear, to stay out of trouble. Kids learn strategy very early. The power kids have is underrated and taken for granted. He'd say these things to me, and I'd just nod my head to have him think, "ohhhhh...riiiiight... I didn't realize, well I must have gotten it all wrong" when I knew what I knew. But I still had to live with him until my mom came home. This was the best strategy I believed I could take. Just agree for now and keep the peace, until I can make something of myself and then, leave.

Chapter Five: My School Years
Playlist: Taylor Swift – Mean

As an only child of the '70s and '80s with no internet, smartphone or gaming devices to have me gaze away into a pixelated world, I learned to manage my alone time with the more physical games I had.

I played with an '80s robotic, Texas Instruments spelling toy called Speak & Spell. I tried Rubik's cube (and only managed to solve one side, 'til this day). I didn't always have anyone to play along, so I dropped red and black plastic coins into a yellow-holed grid to create pretty patterns and designs instead of connecting four in a row of the same color as the game instructed. I attempted to beat Simon but found myself punching the lit-up buttons as if I were in a back-alley fight – always ending with me yelling into the sky like how Charlie Brown from *The Peanuts* did, accepting failure every time.

I was blown away by the accuracy of comedian Gilda Radner of *Saturday Night Live*, who played a young girl named Judy Miller. Judy would pretend to be the host of a TV show in her bedroom and play all the roles of the guests that appeared on her pretend show. When the ruckus got to be too much, we'd hear her mom calling out asking her what she was doing, and Judy always answered, "Nothing!" Judy was my spirit sister.

I refocused my attention to simply being on my own and being okay with it. I learned through the years that I'd been given the task of working my tail off on my own for a greater purpose. I used to daydream of a life that would look like the best parts of the shows *The Brady Bunch*, *Happy Days* and the movie *Grease*. I saw many of my friends having a pretty good support system, be it their siblings, one or both parents, grandparents or relatives, and solid friends that showed up with the shit hit the fan. Life looked so good in their world; they lived my daydream while I returned to my reality and saw depression, fights, neglect, silence, sadness, resentment, no support, and a lot of pretending to the world.

There were plenty of times I let the lack of support and encouragement get to me. I wondered why? Why me? I played Karma's justifying card my mom used to play that asked, "What did I do in my past life to deserve this?" I felt an ethereal response spoken in my heart. "...just keep on moving forward."

And that's what I did.

My Bullies

First through fifth grade had some peaks but a lot of valleys for my emotional development. When I think about it I can clearly say holy crap, I was bullied for five years. By different people! In different areas of my life!! All the time!!! FROM EVERY DIRECTION!!!!

Friends recommended me to watch a series of movies based on a character named *John Wick*. In fact, that was the name of the title for the movie that came out in 2014. It's May 17, 2019 and I just finished watching the third chapter of this series in the theater. I had watched the previous two a few months prior and am now all caught up, awaiting the next installment for 2021.

John Wick's world reflected his constant badass energy and his hardcore fight maneuvers and strategies to stay alive among all the assassins targeting him. After seeing the first three installments, I felt an emotional metaphor between John Wick's physical survival from his assassins to my emotional survival within my first five years of elementary school. There was always an emotional battle going on in establishing my right to my identity. In my intangible world, everyone from my parents, babysitters, neighbors, family, teachers, and school community became my emotional assassins.

An article shared online by *Cool Material* discussed that the fight scenes in the movie reflected a style of fighting art called "Gun Fu." It originated by John Woo in the '80s and was used again with John Wick director Chad Stahelski. The art is a mix of

"Japanese jiu-jitsu, Brazilian jiu-jitsu, tactical 3-gun, and standing Judo."

As the article continued, it described the overall experience to be "partially traditional and partially experimental, a style rooted in reality yet punched up for the big screen."
(Credit: https://coolmaterial.com/media/john-wick-gun-fu/)

That's exactly the kind of style someone like myself can relate to, mentally and emotionally. I learn and then I create as I go along, finding what works for the assassins in my silver-screened life.

John wears a suit when he fights. If I could relate to that, my suit would be my smile. John's way of work is to stay focused and get the job done. My outside appearance of "I've got it all together" is my fight suit, while on the inside I'm recovering, moving strategically behind a car and taking out two negative experiences like a pair of assassins.

Pew!Pew!

I look at bullies like assassins. They target you, breaking into your emotional home without any permission, and then they ruthlessly destroy everything that represents what you value and who you are while in there. In my world, there was a teacher who spanked students; she yanked my classmates by the arm, belittled them, and threatened them. She yelled at all of us, and even kept kids from going to the bathroom to the point of peeing on the floor.

There were selected students grossly favored and spotlighted often; they were given freedom to do what other kids would never get the chance to do because the teacher had already picked who would be "sentenced to life" without her respect, encouragement or inspiration. And then there were kids who observed it all, like me, who came to school scared as shit.

I already came equipped with being belittled, yelled at, ignored and spanked because I wasn't fulfilling the unreachable expectations given to me. I already had the loud noises of parents fighting at home still clamoring in my ears — the echoes of their disappointment in each other, and in me. I already had relatives finding fault and segregating me because I was American, and they weren't.

I already had the "hit-first-ask-questions-later" style of parenting that had me afraid to ever say a word, voice a thought, share an opinion, or claim a discovery worthy of sharing. I was perfectly suppressed like a good girl needed to be so the outside world can tell my parents what a sweet child I was. I wasn't about to tell a soul what was happening in my classroom. I was simply going to keep my head low and aim to please so I can get through each class without any beating of any type.

I couldn't handle the additional fear of fitting in. I spent most of my first grade throwing up every morning before heading to school. Can you imagine if I upset my teacher, and she told my parents? Screw that. I'd rather throw up, go to school and find survival strategies to keep her from targeting me.

Ever notice just how many ways there are to be bullied? According to StopBullying.gov, there are four: Verbal, social, physical, and cyber.

When we think of bullies, imagine - who bullies us? Bullies come in all shapes, sizes, and demeanor. They don't all have that mean-streak look in them. They can be moms and dads, grandmas and grandpas, aunts and uncles, brothers and sisters, teachers and instructors, classmates and friends.

When I recognized this, it had me thinking of the author of horror and sci-fi novels, Stephen King. He brought subjects that would usually be considered as safe in the hearts of adults and children, and then with a demonic twist, change that whole image up in our imagination. The amazing St. Bernard (*Cujo*). A healing nurse (*Misery*). A funny clown (*It*). They turned into nightmares. Not just unsafe, but full-on emotional, mental anguish, physically torturous and fatal. Do a Google search on those to learn more. My point is that you don't always know what you're going to get in the social world you step into.

Third grade. Enter stage right, the fifth-grader assassins. I never caused trouble. Never spoke back. Never invited trouble. I just followed directions through elementary school. I was under so much control that I only knew to follow and obey, accessorized with a sizeable fear of ever letting anyone down.

In third grade, a group of fifth graders followed me home every day for two years (yes, that means even when they were sixth and seventh graders in another school, they actually returned to find me). They would tailgate me as I walked home, talking purposefully loud to one another about how unbelievably ugly and stupid I was, being Indian. I was, to them, a "stupid Hindu." The color of my skin was like the color of shit, and shitty people should be flushed away.

Every aspect of an Indian person that they could imagine was intensely belittled and deconstructed. I was so stunned that they even had an imagination and vocabulary that was that horrible, saying the most terrible things to someone who simply existed. They painted the most frightening pictures in my young mind about how they felt about me. I never looked at them in school, never knew them or their friends, and never hurt them. I never imagined anyone in school could actually enjoy doing something like that as a pastime on a daily basis. Actually, wanting someone they don't know to leave, be beaten, run over, raped, murdered. Ugh. It was an ugly time to be me. I can understand why kids today make decisions to leave this place, even when I know it's not the correct decision. I can understand the equation that a kid might have:

They want me gone, so I'll leave =
they'll leave me alone and they'll be happy again.

I can truly empathize.

According to this gang of girls, I needed to go back to the country where I came from because I was too ugly to be here. Okay... so, um, I was living in Skokie, Illinois, United States. If I went back to where I came from, I'd be going back to Chicago, Illinois.

Still the United States.

What's even more interesting? The leader of the pack? Who chanted my need to return to where I came from? She's Asian.

This wasn't a White Power movement, people. This wasn't white against color. This was a group of girls of several ethnicities, targeting me because I'm Indian. By the time I entered fifth grade, I hated being Indian more than ever.

I didn't think so hard about where they came from or anything like that. I was kind of like a Crayola 64-crayon box with the built-in sharpener: I welcomed everyone, no matter who they were, where they were from and wanted the best for them. That's it. Everyone was just a girl or a boy. Only in college did I actually realize that I had friends in grade school who were Mexican, Jewish, Filipino/a, Chinese, Japanese, Korean, Cuban, Israeli, Armenian, Greek, Russian, Polish, Italian, Serbian, Iranian, and Indian. When I think about it, wow, despite the bullying stuff, I was pretty blessed to be surrounded by a demographic that represented a slew of ethnicities and religions. We kind of had the whole world in our educational neighborhood, and like I had said before, I had some peaks I still appreciate, but my valleys felt like an emotional civil war more than peacetime on my battlegrounds through grade school.

I mentioned the movie *John Wick* earlier. Maybe you imagined that I kicked people's asses. Remember that my experience was explained to be more about the intangibles like psychological and emotional. I didn't retaliate that way.

John was never unscathed. He was beaten. Bleeding. A mess. But he got back up and hobbled forward. His skin was bruised, punctured or torn, and blood seeped out through his clothes. But his mind. Oh, his powerful mind. His mind was so powerful that it never understood "game over." It only knew, "game on."

He decided when it was over. And what I admire most about him, is that he never made a lot of noise about anything. He practiced a great level of self-control. He stayed conservative in his position and fought more quiet, productive fights. He remained focused on doing everything he could, reaching every resource he had and pushing forward as powerfully as he could toward his freedom. These attributes are very similar to the type of emotional, self-defense, "kid-survival-Fu" I incorporated, within me.

I spent a lot of time observing social behavior around me. Because of my circumstances, I had a lot of time to think on my own. I was curious about how society reacts to little burps and hiccups in life to grand mall seismic calamities. I'd then focus on successful leaders in society, to see if there was a difference, and there was. Their reactions were impressive.

The reactions of society, in general, were so emotionally soaked in fear, wrapped in anxiety, conditioned to complain and fault-find. The reactions of leaders handled their issues with a process that kept their emotions under more control, and logic in the forefront. I saw that emotionally successful leaders didn't quickly react with emotion first. They looked at the logic before they dispensed any emotional energy to it.

Questions like:

- What happened?
- What caused it to happen?
- What or who were all involved/accountable?
- What options were available?
- What's needed immediately?
- What's the best solution for now?
- What's the best solution for the long run?
- What's the lesson learned?

Of course, situations are emotionally charging, and as humans, our emotions are the most spellbinding influence of all powers we have within our design. I'm going to say that again:

Our emotions are the most spellbinding influence of all powers we have within our design.

Knowing this, it's a shame that our world has spent less time healing, growing, supporting and building outstanding emotions. Scientifically speaking, we are one species, on one planet, in one solar system, of one galaxy, among one hundred billion galaxies in the observable universe. As of right now, according to space.com, there are even some good physics studies that aim toward the possibility of there being multiverses. What am I saying here? I'm saying that there's a tremendous opportunity to actually have a beautiful world and live a quality life, but too many people are either living with a lack of gratitude or settling for a low-quality life with unproductive habits and assumptions in the space we're in (literally and figuratively). I don't suspect most of the population has ever really recognized that we're the only ones here as we know it, rotating along the gravitational pull that allows us to feel grounded on a spherical anomaly. It just takes one false move by any part of the solar system and buh-bye big blue marble and friends. So, what exactly are we doing with the time we're blessed to have?

My mission here is not to fear-monger gloom and doom readers here, or in our society. I just happen to see so much beauty still left in this world, even though the ugly that tends to show up from time to time. There is potential exponential beauty that's been glazed over by emotional injustices that domino behaviors into a downward spiral of continuous unhappy outcomes. People suffering through changes, loss, or poor behaviors of others might not be aware of what they can do for themselves to live a higher quality life from the inside out. They've lost their steam. Misplaced their personal powers. Decided to give up the dream, whatever that is.

There are incredible happenings taking place daily that go unnoticed: miracles, healing, love, humanity for people, care for animals and preservation of our Earth.

I see a lot of good, great and breathtakingly beautiful. Hear incredible stories. So many of them.

But that doesn't offer profit for the ads on television for certain industries and special interest groups. It doesn't get ratings high enough for a demand to showcase more good words and behaviors for children, teens, adults, and overall society. People like and demand drama, controversy, and conflict over that everything-is-beautiful feeling.

I can understand why that happens: the difference is interesting to us. Dramatic events influence the Good Samaritan within us to come together to help, rescue, and love. The only problem I'm seeing is that the default behavior feels like it's shifting to a more disengaged human toward one another than not. Yes, we do have beautiful people in this world, but we're living in lack when there are millions suffering around the world with stress, anxiety, depression, addictions, and other emotionally connected hardships that can be rehabilitated, avoided, and overcome.

We're told in our childhood, how we should never let history repeat itself, yet children continue to witness and experience adults repeating history, passing painful, hurtful, dysfunctional batons down through generations. How, then, can our own children ever perceive that anything will ever actually get better among human love and existence?

For four decades, I've witnessed and experienced a lot of unhealthy, toxic, dysfunctional emotional abuses from a variety of people in my life. But I also saw successful leaders show me two important behaviors that influenced me to contribute to a better-quality life:

1. *They focused on being proactive.* They stepped forward. They thought things through. They scheduled their day to accomplish their needs. When they didn't know an answer, they owned that temporary moment and researched or connected with someone to find their answers.

   They asked questions, communicated, confronted, and concluded. They took responsibility, accountability, and offered apologies when necessary to honor their obligation to a setback. Imagined worst-case scenarios, planned for the worst (plan B) and maintained a level of self-control and self-respect that had people within their circle, community, supporters, students and acquaintances respecting them for not only what they brought to the table, but who they were as a person.

2. *Most of what they do is done by choice.* The choice is our greatest spiritual, emotional, intellectual, and physical superpower. Its power can bring peace, love, and harmony among everything and everyone. The abuse of it can bring destruction and devastation.

The neglect of it can bring chaos, damage, pain, loss, melancholy, and a stagnancy of growth. Successful people consider prioritizing and categorizing their choices, weigh the pros and cons, then turn smaller decisions into routines, and allow time via "sleeping on it" for the more complex decisions. They take responsibility and accountability of the choice they make, and often they're self-driven predetermined decisions. They keep the tool of delegation in their back pocket for matters that either don't require their exclusive investment in the task or when the task is not something that they're experts at handling.

3. I remember learning a simple act through, a fun, self-development book called, *Why Your Life Sucks: And What You Can Do About It* by Alan Cohen: Don't put energy into things that deaden you. It made so much sense, and it's what smart leaders do to free their power and space for their higher priority decisions.

According to a commercial for a Microsoft To-Do App it seems that the number of choices we make on an average day, hover around 35,000. 35,000 decisions! On average!

(Credit: *MicrosoftOffice365*
https://www.youtube.com/watch?v=6k3_T84z5Ds)

Imagine this: while our body moves and processes like a machine, the moment we wake from our sleep we're immediately in choice-mode. Unconscious and conscious. We don't just make momentary, impulsive, and temporary types of choices. We have the power to go as far as using choice to create habits and routines, and soon the outcome of decisions like that influence the quality of our thinking, our efforts, and how confidently and successfully we respond.

Choice holds the power to change everything. Think about some massive decisions made in your lifetime. I remember as a high schooler in 1987, I watched President Regan make a public demand about a certain wall that divided East and West Berlin since 1961 to be torn down. And while I give huge respect to President Regan for fueling the fire, it was the choice and actions of Mikhail Gorbachev (General Secretary of the Communist Party of the Soviet Union from '85 – 91) to make it happen and speed up the process. And it was brought down two years later in 1989, without bloodshed.

I can also think of two incredibly known choices in the New Testament that affected millions of people:

1.   In all four gospels, Matthew, Mark, Luke, and John: Barabbas.

2.   Gospel of Luke 23:34 – "Father, forgive them for they know not what they are doing."

The world's great mentors, inventors, and influencers prove that we all have it in us to grow past old behaviors, ideas, and habits that history tried to define for us. And yes, while spectators like myself, watched leaders perform impressively within their own powers, it's now really important to recognize that we also have powers of our own that are longing to be recognized and used for the greater good.

Successful people commit to valuable practices that help them gain as well as maintain their level of achievements. They develop systems, disciplines, and codes, and train themselves to turn strategies and thought processes into a default standard, staying true to honoring what works and learning from what doesn't work.

Over the decades, I discovered that intellect is important to have, but emotional power is the driver that brings people to higher standards, quality living, stronger relationships, improved physical health, fulfilled mental health and an overall deserved confidence that speaks within our energy saying, "yeah, baby, that's how it's done."

Emotional power is the lost treasure to personal development and fulfillment. Everyone is looking outside for this hidden wealth, and often never finding it; they're left running in angst on that hamster wheel waiting for change to come.

Stop running.

Jump off that wheel.

It takes more than intellect to win in life. It takes more than thinking smart. It takes proactive decision-making, self-controlled powerful delivery and determined consistency. And the only way for those to get engaged and stay engaged is by training for successes through your emotional power.

Remember my discussion about *John Wick* earlier; the character exhibited those mentioned behaviors in stellar fashion, being able to save his life from three men in a bar, using a pencil. That kind of badass win takes emotional power.

In many ways, great leaders in every arena who reflect positive, impressive wins over hard challenges and conflicts actually metaphorically play the role of *John Wick* in the way of emotional power. And that, of all things, impresses me the most.

Chapter Six: My Emotional Albatrosses
Playlist: Don't Let Me Get Me – P!nk

It never mattered what age I was; I was constantly told to respect our elders and forgive our youngsters. And of course, while I understood the point of it, I still wondered – at what point will I be supported when either of those sides wrong me? When an adult beat and/or verbally tries to convince me that I'm useless? When a child takes something of mine and destroys it? When someone older than me betrays me? Or insults my mom? Or me? When someone younger than me lies, hurts me, and affects my reputation?

Don't be angry. Forgive them. Oh, that's okay. They do these things. Just say you're sorry. Even if they did it. Honey let it go. Let your aunt, uncle, teacher, boss, cousin, schoolmate, kid at the park, friend of a friend just do whatever they did and let it be. Karma will take care of it.

Who the hell is Karma, and why can't I just share how messed up they are to do that to me? I often would feel like if there were a court, the grown-ups and the children would all have representation but me? I'd have to represent myself. No question. I was beaten up verbally, psychologically, emotionally, and physically from every type of person in my life. And those who hurt me never had to apologize. They never felt the stings of poor behavior. They just got away with it, while I had to live forgiving it.

I learned *please, thank you, I'm sorry, I was wrong, it's not your fault, I feel bad and please don't be mad at me* as my default language, and the result from that effort was the feeling of being emotionally thrown away, instead of embraced.

Somewhere underneath all of those messages, I slowly came to think that this is everyone's definition of love to me. I thought I was going to lose it because I never believed that love was supposed to feel this way.

I felt that according to their bottom line, I wasn't worthy or valuable, and all I had going for me to keep me from any further drama would be to at least behave nicely through it.

I felt surrounded by bullies who won all the time. "But, wait! Yeah, but... but!!!" was all I heard myself say as I attempted to either explain, defend, or clarify, but no one really cared to hear the reasoning for my rebuttals. It felt as if the only agenda was to shoot me down to win something out of it.

A mental barrage of comments collected from negative commentary seeped into the cracks of my mind and staged a coup in my emotional landscape over the years:

Don't be ugly.
Sit properly.
Don't laugh so loud like that.

Why are you so skinny?
You've put on some weight.
Don't eat so much.

You're the color of shit.
Go back to where you came from.

You should just die. It would be better for the world.
I hope someone rapes you a thousand times daily.

Why don't you eat enough? Eat more.
Don't answer like that; answer like this.

You will lose.
You'll never amount to anything.

I used you, yes, I don't want you anymore.
You're useless.

I hope you get in a horrible accident
and lose everything you worked hard for.

Things change; people change.
Nobody will be there for you.

Do you think they love you?
No one's going to love you.

No one will ever meet your standards.
Why does your skin look dirty?
I'm not sure why I don't like you, maybe it's because
you're Indian.

*I told my family and friends you were Italian; I didn't
want them to know you were Indian.*

I don't have time for your shit.

*You'll never have what it takes.
Beautiful? Really? I don't see it.
You're standard. Average.*

*5'8" and 128? Not good enough.
Lose twenty pounds, and we'll talk to you.*

No man will ever want to marry you.

*You're so dramatic.
You're so emotional.
You're so sensitive.*

*You know we can always find someone better than
you.*

The collection above scrapes only a fraction of what
I've heard from relatives, friends, teachers,
acquaintances, parents, bosses, managers,
neighbors, etc. I've heard comments like these and
a ton more from grade school to current from people
whom I loved, valued or respected at some point in
my life; those whom I'd gladly go out of my way to

show my loyalty, friendship, and respect.

People who I'd never imagine uttering words like that to try to diminish someone's sense of self or worth. Spotlighting a negative, personal opinion, that would disrespect the existence of someone I cared about is just not my thing.

These continuously unsavory actions toward me eventually paved a hard road in defining what I began to think was their definition of Anita. And over time and continuous repetitive, negative commentary, I started to let the words take over me.

Since all the hard words began before Kindergarten and continued consistently through the years, by the time I reached my early 20's my mind slowly began to plummet into a new belief of myself.
I used logic to justify the equation that the constant collection of commentary must all hold some truth. Maybe they're actually all correct? I might see myself as a good person, but maybe I've got it all wrong, and I really am this albatross to everyone around me.

My father did say I was a liability, not an asset. He is a smart man. Everyone believes he is. Maybe I've got this all wrong.

Maybe I really am a liability.

Chapter Seven: My Enough
Playlist: F**kin' Perfect – P!nk

I looked in the mirror one morning and wondered, "Really? Am I *that* horrible? Useless? Unworthy? Valueless?"

A collection of unhappy moments flashed through my mind like a nightmarish montage. Echoes of the various dialogs that darkened my spirit over the years that I had contained within my steel-vaulted memory slithered out from some crack in my emotional wall. It re-infected me by collectively answering my questions in one single, haunting, whispered sentence,

"Yes, you are."

From the time I was very young, I had a brilliant warrior at my side: my ego. She was amazing. She came in like a brave superhero, saving my Spirit's demise far too many times. She was my emotional bodyguard, who manned the forts of my troubled heart; my life's only emotional survival tool that kicked into gear as soon as I left my house to take on the day. Any time I was made fun of, pushed around, laughed at, criticized, or left alone, my ego appeared like a glowing med kit craved by gamers in the first-person shooter games. I stayed safe behind her, and admirably watched her perform.

She worked hard. Very hard. She had strategies and tactics she'd pull out from secret areas of my brain that held gold. Areas I never knew existed. Gold I could never seem to find on my own.

I don't know how many of those whom I've ever crossed paths with ever really knew who they were talking to when they freely judged, slapped their thoughtless opinion, or comfortably spoke about the oddities or strangeness of me. I don't know if they ever realized how their words impacted hearts like mine, and how they contributed to seducing me into accepting their seemingly collaborative message:

You're just not valuable enough to be respected and loved back.

I remember learning "If you can't say anything nice, don't say it anything at all." Isn't that how it went? Did I get that wrong? Because too many people of all ages, ethnicities, and religions have said or done some pretty terrible things to me, regardless of my youth or seniority, and irrespective of my heart.

And what did I do? I "dealt with it." I followed the rules. When I did wrong, I apologized. When they did wrong, I apologized.

When I questioned anything and wanted to understand their point of view before deciding to change mine, I was accused of being an arguer. A fighter. A quality I loved about my mom, and yet she, too, was shunned from the home, community, education, and work environment I was in.

When I shared my hopes, dreams, and vision for goals, I was laughed at and told that no one will ever rise up to my standards. And when I slowed down my pace, I was too slow.

What are you waiting for?
Why didn't you just go for it?
You wasted time!
You could have had this!
You would have gotten that!

#OhmydearGodInHeavenPleaseStopThis

ENOUGH!!

To survive, I'd respond with a forced smile, displaying the reluctant but required acceptance to something I didn't understand nor agree to. Why did I do that?

I wanted to keep the peace, instead of making waves. It was a strategic decision.

I was an emotional prisoner of a dysfunctional mental war between those who wanted to control me, and my desire to have freedom from their control. Some battles you win by staying silent, keeping your head down and waiting 'til the moment comes to escape or leave. Deep inside, I knew who I was. I believed I was enough.

My stormy connections reflected opportunists entering my warm and sunny days. They'd ask for my time and help, and then sucked all the energy, emotion, and effort out of me. In return, they'd reciprocate by criticizing, judging, and *poof!* they'd disappear, figuratively flipping me the finger and skipping happily away, out my life, unscathed. I came to name these types of bait-and-switchers, Lifesuckers.

Lifesuckers are those who quickly try to position themselves to be close to you, impacting you early on in the friendship. The immediate intention of togetherness is established but eventually plays out to have you honor their eventual expectations of constant attention and satisfaction, on their terms. The message undertone becomes "Do this for me, and I'll approve of you." Quite authoritarian, and narcissistic, but it's delivered in a clever setup: "You're the only person I can trust who knows me, who I can depend on. I need you. Can you help me?"

You fall for the cunning preamble because you're an empathically good person who has a kind heart by design and you are glad to comply. Your relationship appears to hold bonding power at first, but for Lifesuckers, it's an opportunistic manipulation, risking an emotional robbery and a physical heist of our time and effort.

After a while you begin to feel bad, but you justify the negative moments and feelings from them taking advantage of you. Like a snake oil salesman who sold you with great fanfare a bottle of liquid feces, you lovingly supported it, bought it, opened it and boom – shit blasted in your face. You're left in the shower, cleaning someone else's mess and feeling overwhelmingly used and deflated, as if the life was sucked out of you.

Yep. Lifesuckers. That's exactly what they are, and I've had plenty of training in that arena. Their toxic highs and stabbing, apathetic lows mimic the abusive relationship very well because *newsflash * it is abusive! Their unnecessary criticisms, control, betrayals, envy, and jealousy, all eventually placed me on a road to poor self-awareness and bad choices in relationships.

Choices that nearly cost me my life.

What I stubbornly and passionately hungered for was respect and acceptance in who I was, as I was. I couldn't put my finger on what was causing this whirlwind that has me constantly engaging in emotional self-defense. Is it industry standard in an Asian-based world, that a child is expected to bend in all directions to satisfy parental and familial expectations? Or maybe, this affects all ethnicities?

Or maybe, it happens to all first-generation immigrant children?

I didn't know then, and I'm not so sure I even know now. I do, however, know what my mom told me when I was twenty-three:

"You're a sweet, graceful, but strong flower in the middle of everyone else's storm."

I didn't get it then as much as I get it now.

Chapter Eight: My Spirit Flower ✿
Playlist: Flower Child – Lenny Kravitz

My mom painted a picture in my mind with those words:

"You're a sweet, graceful, but strong flower in the middle of everyone else's storm."

Metaphorically, I saw myself as a lotus flower in a shallow, murky pond when it felt like everyone else hung out in the pretty, organized flower gardens.

The lotus was always my all-time favorite flower. I hadn't even known its blossoming design and representation until my 30's. Before then, I just loved it because I marveled at its beauty floating on the water. It seemed magical.

I owned an event planning company over 20 years ago and did a little research on flowers as I was helping a bride-to-be find the best flowers to represent her for her wedding bouquet. I found a flower book and came across the lotus: my jaw dropped. Reading the descriptive details of the incredible flower, not only blew my mind, but the metaphors that came from this flower moved me to tears.

I've collected about ten facts that I learned over the years combined with information obtained by a study on the lotus done by a woman named Share

Siwek. Of all the research I observed on the internet's bazillion reference points, the one thorough study I found was sourced from Share, who lives in the Midwest (like me), in Illinois (like me), in Chicagoland (like me), in the Northwest Suburbs (like me), only about 20 minutes from me. No coincidences. I've already put a call in to meet her.

Credit: http://www.flowersociety.org/lotus-plant-study.htm

1.   The lotus starts out at the bottom of a muddy, murky pond and eventually breaks through to the surface, then bursting in bloom out of the water, airing its beautiful fragrance. By afternoon it begins to make its way toward closing its blooms and sinking under the water. Once the sun goes down, so does the lotus, back into the bottom of the pond, only to rise again out from the muddy waters and back to the surface the next morning, unharmed.

It defies logic, returning into the pond's life below the surface, and re-emerging every day the same way. As I get older and look back, I can see this as a beautiful representation of its will to live, regardless of its circumstances. And the darker, muddier and murkier the water, the more beautiful the flower becomes. This is the ultimate flower of power for hope, inspiration, possibility, defiance, protection – and love.

2.   The roots are buried in the mud, and the stalks of the leaves and flowers are firmly attached to the root, resisting the tug of human hands to pull them out without cutting them.

3.   Lotuses prefer still water of lakes and ponds. They seem to need the mud to get a strong foothold. The Midwest (where I live) is full of dense clay and tenacious mud.

4.   The Lotus embodies all four elements. The plant springs from the mud (Earth) and must be firmly rooted there. Water is necessary to sustain the plant, and the stalks are hollow and filled with milky sap when growing. The leaves and flowers rise from the depths and are held above the water's surface, representing Air. Also, the orientation of the leaves and flowers until they dry is upward, reaching into the air. The air spaces within the stems maintains buoyancy. The flowers and leaves unfurl, representing transformation or Fire.

5.   The lotus lives in both worlds, the physical and spiritual, and represents the ultimate ability to be of service on all planes of existence.

6.   After thousands of years of dormancy and drought, the seeds can still germinate and sprout into plants.

7.   Sacred and divine flower in many religions, most notably Hinduism, Buddhism, and the Baha'i faith.

The Lotus rises from the mud, untouched and clean, to open into a magnificent flower high in the air. The life cycle, stature, and perfection of the Lotus is perhaps the reason that it represents purity, peace, transcendence, enlightenment, rebirth, beauty, and fertility. The flowers open with the light of the sun and close with darkness. Each day is a new life, a new rebirth for the flower. The life cycles of the Lotus evoke how the human spirit unfolds from humble beginnings in the mud to the blossoming of the soul in the ether and light.

8.   The Baha'i temple in New Delhi was designed in the form of a Lotus by the architect, Fariburz Sahaba. He said, "The Lotus not only has an association with all the religions of India but is probably the most perfect flower in the whole world. It is symmetrical; it is exquisitely beautiful. And how does it grow? It grows in a swamp, and it raises its head out of the slime absolutely clean and perfect. Now, this is what the manifestation of God is in the world."

9.   It is the national flower of India (heyy 😊)

10. In yoga, the classic meditation position is called "padmasana" or Lotus position. It is said to help keep the back straight for the transmission of energy through the spine and to help reach the highest level of consciousness. This symbolizes "reaching for pure knowledge while being rooted in the material world of experience."

When I was growing up, we sat "Indian style." I never imagined this term would later be considered offensive to the Native Americans, but that's probably because I thought Indian style was talking about me and my peeps. I grew up sitting that way to eat on the floor, even if we had a table. It was the traditional way to eat.

My grandmother on my father's side taught me that we sat on the floor and we ate with our hand, so the connection from Earth to ourselves, and ourselves to the food we're given is all done in one conscious experience.

Back then, I was like, #YeahOkWhatever, but in my 20's that transformed into #omgThatIsSoProfound. We sat Indian style. Not "criss-cross applesauce" as we might hear from leaders of littles today to keep things politically correct.

When I'd randomly visit India, a family member would either engage me in a moment with yoga or learn Indian dance with their instructor, and I'd hear the word padmasana shared by the instructor as I was standing and I would see the people around me sit down on the floor. I presumed it meant to sit Indian style.

Knowing the real reason of sitting in lotus position today being fully about the transmission of energy through the spine changed my perspective, had me remember my grandmother's words of our union between our Earth, nutrition and body energies, and it lit my thinking up to appreciate the actual power of something as subtle as sitting.

I've been meditating in some way now since my 20's and the lotus is definitely a divine attribute to be deeply appreciated.

So much of the lotus's characteristics mimicked characteristics within my own mental development, inspiration, and behavior. Like the flower being strongly embedded in its roots within the ground, I'm also strongly embedded by way of passion for reaching the direction I want to reach, despite the mud and murky water. Most of my moves are calculated to protect my heart, but once I feel safe, and the coast is clear, I bloom clean and clear to share my heart. I'll share all I can and how I can to heal anyone through their suffering, and when darkness falls, so do I – possibly due to having an empathetic heart. I fall and stay in that darkness to allow my emotions the journey it needs, and then I can rise back again to offer my heart.

It was as if the lotus walked into my heart, deep in the valley of my emotional mountain range, and gave me a congratulatory fist-bump into her secret society that I had always been a part of, but needed to complete the missions before realizing who I really was. I couldn't believe this flower went through physically what I went through emotionally on a daily basis. If there was one flower in the world that I have the utmost respect for the power it has, and the connection it has to me, it would be the Sacred Lotus.

My message to you is to find that spiritual representation of you through a plant, flower, or animal that will help you see the beauty and difference of who you are and the importance of the gifts of power you were given.

Chapter Nine: My Silver Linings
Playlist: Keep on Movin' – Caron Wheeler and Soul II Soul

Powers of the Life Survival Serum: Lessons & Blessings

Since I was a kid, I always felt like I knew who I was, and I found life poetic and metaphoric through nature. Maybe, it's due to being an only child with a limited social life as a kid, but my creative imagination played a part in helping me find ways to go through the maze and get my cheese. I saw myself pausing to pay attention to the message beneath the message, to what the body language told me in spite of what the words said.

I began looking in the eyes of people I talked to, and it revealed more to me. It revealed how they felt more than how they thought. I noticed the energetic connections we attract to and deflect from, and it all boiled down to this mental "life-survival serum" made of two strong and valuable ingredients: lessons and blessings. The older I became, the more valuable the two ingredients have become. And when we place gratitude into those two outcomes, growth in the quality of life takes place.

I realized, for my survival, that if I turned my focus to all the lessons and blessings I'd gain, life could transform and become an adventurous series of unforgettable relationship experiences that I have the privilege to explore.

Everything that posed itself as an issue, soon had me imagine myself as either a detective who can't wait to find the wrench thrown into the machine, or as the movie character *Indiana Jones*, who just entered a new adventure, or the television character, scientist Sam Beckett, of the '90s show, *Quantum Leap*, whose backdrop changed in his life and now he had to embark on a new mission to conquer. I think I was the only one who felt that way.

I felt like I was a free spirit within a family structure where my mom was anchored to traditional, cultural and religious expectations, and my father followed a specific equation to financial success, fulfilled the intellectually-required basic duties of a husband and father, and who believed that love was purely conditional.

Power of Music

In 1989, I heard the message again to keep on moving, but this time on the radio. The song was actually called "Keep on Movin'" and it was sung by a group called *Soul II Soul*, featuring *Caron Wheeler*. That groove hit the mark for me and was the background music when I'd hit the valleys of my emotions. Music always moved me. I connected to music of all kind. From the morning and weekend music of my parents who listened to ragas from Ravi

Shankar, memorable songs from Bollywood singers like Lata Mangeshkar, and South Indian gems of temple-style songs in Sanskrit by Yesudas – to the top 20 radio hits of Chicago's B96, Classic to Hard Rock songs of Q101 and New Wave, House music, Reggae, Ska, Country, big bands, Frank Sinatra, even orchestra/classical music - if the sound made me move, groove, dance, tell a story or feel inspired, I was down with it.

My parents found it amusing that I caught on to the jingles of commercials and, what's funny is that I never really paid attention to what I was singing. I just sang it because it sounded cool.

Whether it be a cinematic orchestra, a piano played in the mall, or the songs we heard on the radio, music found its way to move me. It has the ability to actually be my glorified emotional therapist, who sits down with me when I don't want to get back up and relates with me. It fights for me. It helps me sleep. It tells me stories of wins and losses in love. It gives me advice, it hugs my heart, and it motivates me to step out of my 7 hours and 15 days of being a bird without a song, and launches me right into the danger zone, where I reconnect, with my need for speed, in catching up to where I last left myself, with missions to accomplish.

Music was one of the only ways I could express how I felt about something, how someone made me feel, or helped me dream about a big moment, like meeting the perfect boy, or fantasize about walking the runway with mega supermodels *Cindy Crawford* and *Linda Evangelista*. Or imagining Danny Zuko of the T-Birds in *Grease* coming over to my house with his automatic, systematic, hyyyyydromatic car, telling me it didn't work out with Sandy and that he dug brunettes better because he had dark hair, too (why not, it's my daydream).

At this time in high school, I was in a secretly depressed place. My parents fought a lot and I felt like a burden to them. They were talking about divorce, which led me to quit the band. I didn't want to quit, but the pressure I felt wasn't allowing me to practice, my grades were slipping, and friends shifted around. Things didn't feel so great, even if I played it off as they did. All I could do at that time was play my mixtapes that had Soul II Soul singing: ♫Keep on movin'. Keep on movin' don't stop, no. Keep on movin'♫. I believed that was the only point I needed – to keep on movin' when shit decides to hit the fan again.

And it, damn it, it did...

Chapter Ten: My Senior Year
Playlist: Creep – Radiohead

Senior year was an uneasy year for me, contrary to any of my classmates' belief. My mom was depressed over my father and the dysfunctional lonely life with him. And I ended my time in band. It was the first year watching the marching band practice outside, and on the field, and I wasn't a part of it. The whole thing felt weird.

What was weirder was the next unbelievable happening in all of humankind: I was elected to be on homecoming court. That was the shock of all shocks for me, especially next to the girls who were on the court with me. I just didn't fit in. I knew all of them, but they – they were popular! They were ALL popular. I hear from a lot of classmates today that they swear I was popular according to them, and I honestly don't see it that way. I don't know how exactly they came to that, unless the equation of poms uniform = popular, but that wasn't me. I wasn't a part of the popular crowd. I knew them, and said hi to them, but I wasn't popular. What I was, was someone who joined the volleyball team, the dance troupe, DECA, Band, Marching Band, Color Guard, AND poms over four years. I practically tried out for or joined every single thing I could.

I looked at the girls in Homecoming Court with me: they all were at a completely different level than me. I can't explain it, but they were. I just felt like slithering away and watching this unfold from the stands.

Assembly time came, and the votes were in. I can't even remember if the whole school was in the gym or if it was just the seniors, but let's just say there were a lot of people present to find out who the 1990 Homecoming Queen was going to be. The teacher walked up to the mic and began to announce. The previous Homecoming Queen was present with the crown to place on the next winner. And then it happened. As the winner was being revealed:

"1990's Homecoming Queen is..."

Everything moved in slow motion.

"Aaaa – niii – taaa..."

They announced my name.

ME?? Oh my god. What???
They announced MY name.

I was so shocked that I dropped my head into my hands and started to cry. To the crowd, I probably looked like I had a pageant moment, crying tears of winning because that shows humility. Yeeeah-no. These tears had a long, emotionally taxing story that led to feeling overwhelmed in shock that anyone would have considered me.

I still get choked up over that moment.

See, when your environment tells you over and over again since preschool onward that you're not much of anything. When you're always told to sit down and shut up. That you won't amount to much, or your behavior isn't good enough, or your grades are worthless, or you're slapped or yelled at for saying the wrong thing, making a noise, staying awake when you can't sleep, spilling milk, not knowing the answer to a question, giving the wrong answer, being told you don't deserve this, and shouldn't have that, and no matter what effort you put in, something about what you do will be a failure – how is it really possible to believe that anyone would think you're worthy of anything good?

When classmates who make lists at parties of who's prettier, who's ugly, and when the boys look at you and laugh as they write your name under the ugly category, or when bullies in school follow you home to tell you to go back to the country you came from because the color of your skin – over and over again, for years, you can't believe you'd ever hear that about 95% of the same people you've known since kindergarten would EVER elect you to be their

Homecoming Queen. But they did. And boy, let me tell you, I was floored.

I was partly skeptical but mostly grateful. Seeing the slew of friends rush down from all corners of the gym to celebrate and hug me, screaming happiness for me, I have to tell you, it still makes me a little emotional having that memory.

I never imagined I'd ever see the day where anyone would support and care about anything I accomplished. The good stuff that I saw on television as a kid, and among friends and their families just happened to me in one fell swoop. I was incredibly humbled and grateful beyond words.

I know becoming the Homecoming Queen isn't an educational achievement, but there's something to say when your school believes you, among all the coolest, admired kids in your class – you, are their chosen one. And if anyone reading this ever went to a public school, you might agree that social achievements are a surprising relief to have especially if you're told over and over again by your community that your appearance and presence in one way or another doesn't fit the part.

I ran to the payphone by the cafeteria, called my mom, and told her the pretty intense news.

"Oh, yeah?" she responded. "Good, so how is school going? Grades coming along?"

"Yeah, my grades are still fine. But, MA! Did you hear what I said?? The school picked ME. Out of all those amazing girls. I can't believe it! Isn't that CRAZY?!"

"Yah. Ok, Ani, let me go, I have to take care of some things. I'll see you when you get home."

I can't blame her for having the reaction she did. I wasn't experiencing her emotional world. I was living in mine. Knowing that her worry was more about getting the food for dinner done right, so there were no criticisms as he was eating, her worry on maintaining her cultural and religious traditions, her desires to stay in touch with her family in India, and the friendships she is building here for her heart, I would imagine she was more the Homecoming Queen than myself. I'd vote for her every day, and twice on Sundays.

But at that time, in that moment, in my emotional design, I was looking for that excited reaction that we all want from our parents when we accomplish something that feels like a big deal.

It's one thing to be happy for yourself knowing your history of other people's identification struggles with you, but it's another when specific people you care about, who were a part of an experience or moment celebrate 100% with you. Seeing that rush of friends run in from every corner was an amazing moment for me. The feeling was like an electric connection that switched on and lit up the shadowed room in my heart brilliantly.

This felt so incredible and crazy all at the same time, but mind you, this win is *not* viewed as an accomplishment for my Indian parents. I can hear my dad in his Indian accent talk about this:

"What is this... HOMECOMING. Who is coming home? It's all nonsense. Work on your grades. Then we will see who will be coming home. Homecoming. Ha. Shit."

And my sweet but unaware mom who mirrors *All in the Family*'s Edith Bunker in her personality toward my dad responded, "Oh, let her enjoy. This is what they do. It is an American cultural thing. What – you came to America, no? This is what comes with it. Accept it. God only knows what it means, coming home, homecoming whatever, but it is a good thing, huh? Ok, then. Anita, look at me, it's good. Just focus on your grades, ok? That is what matters most. But very good, Ani."

Aghhh. Ok, ma. Thanks.

A classmate in high school showed an interest in me about a month prior to the whole Homecoming moment. I didn't have much of luck in the dating world in high school and was pretty happy to start dating. I may have seen him a couple of times where we just hung out and talked. He was also elected into became the Homecoming King. How perfect! I was just getting to know him and this whole couple thing was starting to feel really nice.

Saturday arrives and I'm performing at the homecoming game with my pom squad. Just before performing, two classmates walked over to where I was standing by the bleachers and started to talk to me with sad faces.

They overheard that homecoming voting was rigged. That they had heard all the boys on the football team tell everyone to vote for me because of the dude that was with me for the month. They said it looked like the votes weren't genuine.

I just stood there with a flood of feelings that had me go back in time, walking the hallways just after the hoopla of my name being announced. I'm recalling all the smiles, congratulations from classmates, etc. My heart sank. Wait, were all the kids who congratulated me in the hallway in on it too? This was all a show? A rigged production for some *MTV Real World* shit, perhaps??

What-The-Fuck?

I felt sick to my stomach. I lowered my head down and looked at the ground. So, this whole thing was a joke.

Sigh Ok.

♫ Keep on movin'♫

I still, for integrity sake, continued the journey and went to the dance with the dude who told me he really liked me. At least I had that going for me. We met up with our friends and went to dinner before the dance. The dance followed, and then the big afterparty at a local hotel. You'd think that would be the best part of the day, regardless of the heavy news two classmates handed me at the game earlier.

From the moment he met with me that night and until the our 1st dance on the dance floor, the King had nothing to say. He exhibited a full disengagement, with no explanation. Couldn't help but recall the story told to me on the field hours before. The story I was trying to forget. But his behavior would make sense, then, if what I heard was true.

I was starting to feel a little paranoid but kept trying to debunk it. I stayed smiling for the yearbook cameras taking pictures of us dancing. I don't like making scenes, and this felt too embarrassing to spotlight the issue when the school was watching us dance. I played it off like all was great. He just stayed the course, chewing his gum and looking around to connect visually with his buddies. He'd stretch and nod his head quickly to the guys he knew as he swayed side to side with me.

The last thing I want is to push anyone to do something they don't want to do when it comes to me. You don't want to hang out with me? Ok. Don't feel like being friends with me anymore? No problem. Don't want to date me? Got it. Don't feel like calling/texting me anymore? Sayonara, Chumley. I'm okay with that. Well, of course I'm not happy about the moment. Of course it hurts.

But I'd rather give freedom to people I care about if they're not willing to work out issues, make wrongs right or keep things transparent to avoid burning bridges that don't need to be burned. No one has an obligation to stay with me. I'm sure the preference in how I handle people who'd "rather not" whatever it is came from the episode in chapter four of this book. Better to let go and wish them well than to hold on to someone who can't see or appreciate your worth.

I only asked him what was wrong once through my smiles, and he responded with one sentence. "I can't wait for *Rob Base* to come on." And that was that.

Okay, then. *Rob Base* and *DJ EZ Rock* were the duo of the hip-hop lyrical times in the late '80s, and, well, if *Rob Base* trumps dancing with a 17-year-old spicy kitten like me, well, then it does. But that wasn't the way I thought in 1989 at the dance. I was feeling more like all of this was hitting me too hard. The moment our dance came to an end I ran to the girl's restroom, locked myself in a stall and cried it out as quietly and quickly as I could.

I was flooded with embarrassment. I believed the two girls all too well at that point. As awful as it seemed, his behavior of a sudden lack of interest was jelling with the story: it would make sense that he was done talking to me. He became king. The hunt is over. He was done with me, and I accepted the disengagement.

I changed gears and set him free as quickly as I could. There was no real investment of time into either of us, so no loss. Funny thing, that *Rob Base* song, "It Takes Two" held some meaning for me. In the end, it does take two to make a thing go right. I wasn't mad at anyone. I think I was just embarrassed to be me. And me, by definition of others, just kind of really sucked.

For the first time, I felt a glimmer of acceptance but learning that it was all rigged, I won't lie to you, the experience sat in my gut and rotted a little more every day for years. I declined to attend the following year to crown the next winner. I didn't attend the ten-year reunion with one of the reasons being that ugly memory.

I was asked later in life why I didn't tell anyone about what happened. My answer was simply why burden anyone with that embarrassing story. I needed to let that go and move forward. I didn't want revenge. I just wanted to move on, and maybe time will heal the experience. And who knows, maybe one day when I'm older I'll write about it. ;)

Chapter Eleven: My Warriors and Healers
Playlist: Freedom90 – George Michael

Later that year, I quit the pom team, and spent most of my senior year during lunch at a friend's house who saw something that most other classmates didn't recognize. Not everyone's equipped to see or pauses the autopilot of school life to actually look at the message behind the eyes. She saw the sadness in my eyes.

I guess the years of stifling, watching, enduring and losing to the ugliness of people takes its toll, and with my parents fighting daily as my home's background soundtrack, it just turned me into a sad girl, playing a happy girl, disguised as a girl who has everything together. But to the ones who can see into the eyes and recognize the truth – to the friend who saw the sadness within my eyes, I'm forever grateful.

She took me aside, asked me what was going on, and listened to my answers. She then softly told me where her house key was hidden, and to go there at lunch break and sleep on her bed. To go recharge enough to get through the day. I'd normally never take that offer because, while it's beautiful, I've never done anything like that – just go to someone's home to rest my head? I wouldn't normally dream of accepting the invitation, as kind as it was. But my eyes reflected a heart that was so sad that I didn't flinch from her offer. In full commitment I said okay, and I left for her house immediately. I found the key, walked into her house, into her room, fell onto her bed, and let my tears marathon their way down my face.

I realized over the decades, when we hit emotional crossroads, we're provided two kinds of Earth Angels: Warriors and Healers.

The warriors are the ones who come into your life resembling something akin to Drill Instructors from your first day entering the USMC Boot Camp in Parris Island. Their purpose is to kick your ass. They'll walk onto the bus that brings the civilians in and begin the work of getting in their face to shock and shake their inner mental makeup.

They hit you hard with their words. They're mean, direct, and want you to feel their emotional earthquake. And in the end, if you can withstand the vocal challenges and learn from their overall intention, you'll either grow stronger from it, or you'll know what you never want to deal with ever again and get out of it.

Warriors show up with the purpose to train you on your own powers. To test you. To push you to survive the mental war, or physical challenges and expectations. You'd think all mean, criticizing, hard-shelled people are awful, but in reality, I like to view 99% of them as warriors who come around to help develop what you want and don't want in your world. They may be obstacles, blocks, detours and challengers. Even the nay-sayers. I'd like to believe they are all here for a purpose to improve us – they only just do things in a very unorthodox way.

The other type is the Healer. This is the empathic person who also enters your world for a reason and a season, providing you emotional nourishment like oxygen for our lungs through his or her comforting words, actions, or resources for our mental respite.

My classmate was a Healer, and while knowing my demeanor would never accept such an offer, taking it was necessary. Most people would feel bad to accept intruding in someone else's home, even if invited in. It's the craziest thing to do, but the truth is, the offer is more important for our emotional survival than rejecting it and continuing life as it slowly unfolds another avalanche of more unsavory experiences.

Infancy through high school, my parents, were struggling to figure out how to live in America with their culture being vastly different than the American culture. They also needed to learn more about each other and how to have a healthy relationship. And they both had to deal with their issues, calamities, and emotional angst mostly on their own because parenting styles were different than what they're becoming today, where everyone's emotional design is slowly (finally) getting acknowledged. Very slowly. But still, it's a start!

In four decades, society's gone from threats and beatings to pausing and giving children a listening ear. Parents are now more accepting of paying attention to the *why* behind their child's behavior. Many leaders are out there now reminding how to parent with peace, but we have a massive population of stressed out, depressed and anxiety-riddled grown-ups. We still have a long way to trek to stabilize the emotionally unstable to balance the scales of the heart, mind, and spirit. Great things will come when more take recognition of the world of cause and effect in the emotional realm.

I don't know if you remember or had a role model as a teen, but I did. While I loved *Janet Jackson* for her coolness, strength, beauty and dancing, and *Sade Adu* for her voice, her quiet sultry maturity and her attire, it's Supermodel *Cindy Crawford* who blew me away.

Cindy Crawford to me is simply gorgeous, classy, and carries a sex appeal that's part girl-next-door and part vixen from another planet. It wasn't just her decency in behavior when she was ever interviewed. Cindy graduated valedictorian from her high school, earned a scholarship at Northwestern University, and went for engineering. When she decided to try modeling, she became a supermodel.

This woman reached the top in everything she put her mind to and soared! Reading about her always impressed me. I loved how she managed the craziness on MTV, with interviews, and the runway.

One afternoon in 1987, I remember being approached by a scout who was from John Casablancas Modeling Agency when I was walking in Chicago with my mom. The scout wanted me to consider joining them. I laughed finding that whole request funny.

Yes, I knew that John Casablancas invented the idea of "Supermodel." And I knew that John Casablancas founded Elite Model Management, one of the world's best modeling agencies ever. But the request to try out their school? That amused me. The Homecoming Queen who felt like the joke of the school, going to a modeling school? Yeah, no. No thanks.

He kept talking, and there was one thing he said that had me completely 180 the decision to an absolute YES. What made me change my mind? They told me *Cindy Crawford* attended that school. Sign me up!

Chapter Twelve: My Heroes
Playlist: My Hero – Foo Fighters

In my earliest years of kindergarten, through the first few grades of elementary school, there were three television shows that I loved. These were shows that made me laugh, think, and cleverly had me learning at the same time. They introduced me to my first heroes:

1.   My very first television hero might surprise you. From kindergarten to about fourth grade a cartoon dude had me appreciate words. His name was "Letterman" from *The Adventures of Letterman* segment, off of the '70s PBS show *The Electric Company*. He had me wishing I could be "faster than a rolling 'o,' stronger than a silent 'e' and able to leap tall T's in a single bound...". He showed me the power of words and the challenge of the sinister Spellbinder who'd always create havoc at the moment by simply changing one letter. I found it so funny and interesting to see what would happen to the situation when one letter-change took place.

2.   The next dy-no-mite *Electric Company* sketch featured a young dude named *Morgan Freeman*, as Easy Reader, who made reading oh, so cool. He'd get so thrilled every time he read a complicated or unique word, that he had me looking for cool words to pronounce, finding words that were a little more special than the standard, common words, to say the same thing. Besides feeling "outta sight!" I felt

smarter and looked forward to his next sketch. Easy Reader became my word hero for showing me the power of words. I think one of the coolest experiences is watching my word hero reach the point of speaking so well over the years that now, with him at 81-years-old as I write this, he's become one of the most recognizable figures in the entertainment industry. He carries an Academy Award, Cecil B. DeMille Award, the recipient of the coveted Kennedy Center Honors, and a slew of awards across the entertainment award spectrum.

He took "easy reading" to a whole other level that turned him into one of the best narrators, actors, and film directors in the film world. As a "first-class genuine readin' freak" he gained staying power remaining at the top of his cool game. This cat is my kind of mentor – right on!

3.   The third hero was absolutely epic, and I still believe one of the most important figures of my lifetime that was underrated when we look at the level of profound power in the simplest gestures that he professed in his teachings and presentation. He was a hero who proved he didn't need a cape to be one. Just maybe a cardigan, and a song. *Fred Rogers*, of *Mister Rogers' Neighborhood*, exemplified what a beautiful human being would look like on television, and off. And yes, while his market was children, he inspired adults as well. He was my undercover trainer who unknowingly taught me the power of kindness, patience, and the

extreme power of imagination. I loved the way he spoke to everyone, even if he had a rejection, declination, or setback; he managed to show his best self through it. It wasn't work for him to show his best self, though. It was his default.

When I work with clients or speak to groups, I'd like to have people focus on what their default behavior looked like. I'll ask you the same. On an average day, what's your nature of being like? Happy? Worried? Frustrated? Melancholy? Cynical? Welcoming? *Mr. Fred Rogers* exhibited respect as his default. He made everyone, I mean *everyone* feel like they were the most important person he's met. He,

- exhibited incredible listening skills

- reflected amazing patience

- entertained without an utterance of a single swear

- didn't have to make big noises to get attention

- shared from his heart and saw the heart in others

- gave us permission to explore our dreams and live in them

- brought value to people that others may otherwise have viewed as "hired help" and nothing more

- saw everybody as a special somebody.

Mr. Fred Rogers viewed a beautiful day in his neighborhood and influenced us to view a beautiful day in ours through acts of kindness, discovery, gratitude, and support. He fought for the love that everyone deserved, and he, in many ways, played a great father-figure role model for my heart since my father was more disengaged in guiding and spending time with me.

Even as I grew older, I recall viewing a 1999 video that shared *Mr. Rogers'* view in learning to handle tragic situations. He said, "When I was a boy, and I would see scary things in the news, my mother would say to me, 'Look for the helpers. You will always find people who are helping'... Because if you look for the helpers, you'll know that there's hope."

Credit: Excerpt from https://interviews.televisionacademy.com/interviews/fred-rogers with gratitude to the Television Academy Foundation.

It was the best fifty-seven seconds of video that shared how to tune out from tragedy and tune in to not just the idea of rescue, healing, helping, but that there are heroes among us. People just like you and me who made a decision to go in and help for the greater good. It doesn't diffuse that bad things happen. His mom's approach was to keep hope in the picture that's being painted in the mind of a developing child (dare I say, I think the message can also be painted in the minds of adults these days). His words inspired me to share his mom's message, as a mom myself, to my daughter – to not only look for those helpers but to aspire to become one of them in the face of conflicts and challenges. *Mr. Rogers,* to me, is my heart hero.

Chapter Thirteen: My Superheroes
Playlist: Superheroes – The Script

The first superhero I ever saw on the silver screen was *Christopher Reeve* in the 1978 movie *Superman*. I was six years old then, but I knew a superhero when I saw one. I remembered the way my heart sighed when he lifted his love interest, Lois Lane, into the air and soared the skies with her. I remembered how my heart sank in another scene, seeing him reach her car only to discover the avalanche from the earthquake consumed her. I remembered my jaw drop seeing him shoot up and out of the atmosphere, and then spin around the planet Earth so fast, he stopped it and spun it in the opposite direction to turn back time, and how my heart flew to the sky when he saved her. And then we all saw him return back as Clark Kent, the regular, everyday human being.

It wasn't turning the time back that had me impressed (though I love time travel stories), it was his desire to do whatever it took on his own to make change happen.

Okay, okay, he was also the first super cute, super kind, a super powerful superhero I ever saw. When I began observing more about the character's structure in the movie, I loved the story even more. I recognized that this character played three roles in one: he began as Kal-El, was named Clark Kent, and became recognized as Superman.

Kal-El to me, represented someone brand new to the world, unsure of his surroundings, and himself.

As Clark Kent, he navigated through his community and society, finding his ways to fit in with the crowd while figuring himself out.

And finally as *Superman*, he learns about his powers, and as he comes to know them, he trains on those powers over and over, ultimately serving his purpose using those powers for the greater good, despite the naysayers, doubters, and villains that try to keep him from his purpose.

I used to wish he'd come to my house like he did for Lois Lane. I remember wishing he could save me. To take me away to a place where I could be me.

Where I didn't feel the pressure to be one kind of Indian that would suit my mother's thoughts, or another kind that would suit my father's thoughts.

Or where I don't have to be anyone else but who I am.

He was indeed the greatest superhero I ever saw who sent me three powerful messages:

1. preserve your inner weirdo
2. keep on moving when things get tough
3. use the powers and talents you were given to use for the greater good.

Back in the late '70s, I used my time after school watching shows on television. I'd throw the TV on and watch cartoons like *Tom and Jerry, Woody Woodpecker* and sitcoms like *Brady Bunch, One Day at a Time, Happy Days, Welcome Back Kotter and What's Happening!* to take me away from the realities that frustrated me and instead bring me to laughter.

One day I came home, finished my homework, grabbed my regular chocolate pudding, and peeled the metal lid open as I saw a show that had a gorgeous brunette who worked very conservatively. She wore glasses and had her hair up in a bun. Suddenly, when a challenge called for help, this reserved lovely stood up and commenced a super galactic power spin a few times, transforming her into an amazing female superhero called, *Wonder Woman.*

Oh. My. Gawd…

Wonder Woman.

I never saw a female superhero before. And wow, she was gorgeous, curvy, intelligent, feminine, strong, assertive, caring, and can only work with the truth. I was blown away. *Wonder Woman* depicted the best definition of a woman I could ever imagine. She instantly became my all-time favorite role model.

I later noticed, *Wonder Woman* had the same set up in her roles as *Superman* did in his. Kal-El was his original name, was given Clark Kent as his alias, and became *Superman* with his powers.

We now have, "Diana, Princess of Paradise Island" as her original name, was given Diana Prince as her alias, and she became *Wonder Woman* with her powers used for the greater good.

I loved the pattern.

I tried to throw my hair into a bun and spin around, hoping I could transform into that incredible woman with her killer outfit and boots. I'd get so dizzy trying I'd stumble and fall on my bed or floor. I leaned on this television show for inspiration, hope, and daydreaming power when life gave me setbacks. The show's theme song still plays in my head every now and again when I feel like I'm on a mission to accomplish, ♫♫ *"Wonder Woman!* ♫ All the world is waiting for you, and the power you possess..." ♫♫

And while I aspired that one day the world might finally see me as an asset and not a liability, I found myself tucking my positive potential into the back pockets of my spiritual jeans when critics older and younger than me found ways to hurt, belittle, deceive and betray me.

Getting on in real life without her literal Lasso of Truth, or her unique bracelets that could deflect the metaphoric bullets shot from lifesuckers, posed a challenge of a lifetime for a growing mind that depended on logic, and a developing emotional heart that depended on reason.

I was getting worn down without knowing how to process, recharge, and rebuild well enough to become stronger for the harder hits that were to follow.

Chapter Fourteen: My S.O.S.
Playlist: Last Breath – Creed

Stress. Overwhelm. Suicide. – Where the most significant power is hidden.

Over my late teens and early 20's, I lived off of a constant level of what I'll call Survival Stress. It feels like you're always emotionally almost drowning on the inside while behaving like life is just fine on the outside to avoid answering the dreaded common question: What's wrong?

Let's be real here, you can have ten thousand plus friends on your social media, know at least one hundred fifty people who wish you a happy birthday and say they think you're pretty awesome, and want the best for you, thirty who might come to a celebration or kick off to support you, five to ten who might call or text you monthly, and anywhere from zero to three friends who might to your voice's response, see a different message in your eyes and drop every fucking thing to save you.

Might.

You might think that people who are at the top of their game have everything they need to stay at the top of their game. That it all came easy because everything always seems to work out okay, according to how you see it. I'm going to call that the *Robin Williams' Effect.*

Try not to get sucked into that perception. The best of the best who reach the best in their lives don't always have it as easy as you think. They work really hard to stay above the water. I can't speak for the details of late comedian *Robin Williams'* reason for letting go of his life, but I can speak of the details that bullied me into almost letting go of mine.

We don't all get the right person at the right time with the right way to keep us from letting go. Not everyone can interpret our pain, our struggle, and not everyone knows our backstory, let alone resonates with our inner emotional design. Sometimes the greatest detectives can't see through the "I'm okay" filter and be present.

And now, in this age with the internet, the signs are even harder to recognize. Everyone can hide behind screens, emojis, acronyms, exclamation points, and cool selfies with fantastic filters. Those things aren't evil, and neither is the internet; they're tools that might be used to help people under emotional pressure who need to preserve a social reputation as they get through their survival stress.

Those who want to live underneath the temptation to let go find ways to ask for help without asking. They send signals out into the world they know:

• The random call from out of nowhere

• The unexpected email/message

- Questions that seem a little bit off

- Change in behavior

If you notice it or have an instinctual or intuitive feeling when you're around someone, I believe that the signal is meant for you to either be there for them or help direct them to the help they desperately need.

In my specific situation, no matter who knew me, no matter what I said, or signal I gave, I believe I wasn't meant to have anyone help me.

I reached a desperate point where I went to a random church and talked to a clergyman. He didn't say anything that talked to my heart. I made a couple of calls to select friends. It just wasn't in the cards when answering machines picked up, and the one who was available naturally focused on sharing what was going on in her life. When she heard just a half of a sentence on what I was feeling, she responded offering the standard apology and wished me well. No one had an idea that the calls I made to them back then was almost the last time they heard from me.

In a short span of a few years, I had felt so buried beneath the surface of the Earth with so many people I cared about holding a dirt-filled shovel and throwing it over me that I began to think that maybe it was time for me to let go:

1. When my father said, "I don't feel like driving to visit you, so you're coming home." and yanked me out of my University when I had just one more year to graduate.

2. When the guy who became my first love cheated on me after two years of what I thought was a strong relationship.

3. When the next man who swept me off my feet, wanting forever, building an amazing relationship with me for a year, and having to break it all off finding out that he never left his girlfriend.

4. When my father secretly bought a house in another State without talking with my mom or myself and expected us to go with him.

5. When I was asked to write and provide a presentation to my father that was to explain how I will live in Chicago since I took a chance to reject his offer to move to Atlanta.

6. When I decided to give my cherished dog to my mom to hold on to him, to keep her company, until I could make enough money to bring her back to me.

7. When I had fallen into the hands of a genuinely horrible guy, who groomed me into his

controlling, possessive, abusive, manipulative, and narcissistic sociopathic ways.

8. When trying to break off the relationship six times, the final time landed me bleeding out in my condo, recovering in the hospital with multiple injuries.

9. When my father pulled me out of Chicago, got rid of my personal things and returned me to their new home in Atlanta.

10. When I had to accept reconstructive surgery for my hearing, and a forced new life in a new location that I didn't favor.

11. When discovering the new life in the new location was even more controlling, with more manipulative moments from an emotionally abusive father who preferred to blame me for my injuries. "What did you do to make him hurt you – you had to have done something."

Eleven significant hardships that took place from '92 - '95.

Stress

Being a college student, whose University was three hours away from home, there was a sense of independence I was able to embrace. But with that independence, followed more responsibilities than I had imagined, especially when it was about maintaining my grades, making new friends, having dating/love interests and still contacting my parents to keep the communication flow regular, for my mom mostly.

At the time, what was interesting to me, was that my highest stress, came from the fear of not gaining approval from my father. Of having him find something wrong in my decisions and activities. In having him form a poor opinion of me based on anything I did or said. Everything else felt like anticipation, excitement, wonder, and discovery. Not stress. But having a father who consistently found ways to deliver whopping news that jolts the mind suddenly makes the pressure not only acute and painful, but the shock in the experience lingers on for years.

When he told me during my 1st semester in my junior year that he no longer wanted me to continue college where I was because he didn't feel like visiting me, that stress domino-effected everything else that had mattered to me. I made new bonds with friends for about three years. I'd have graduated the following year with my degree. I knew the campus well and was comfortable. With his sudden decision, I was now back home, back to his strong rules, his authoritarian attitude, his fights with my mom, and I had to enroll in a new school.

I attended DePaul University for a quarter until my father sprung the new decision to move to Atlanta. The energy of the house was grim, melancholy, and just depressing. Through all the different negative experiences, I managed to find the power to keep myself afloat. At the time, the strength I had was found in burying the ugly stuff that put pressure on me and staying focused on what did work. What was working? The friends that were still around in my life, the good parts of a bad day, and my inner-conversations with the amazing AI; more on AI later.

Overwhelm

We might all reach a point where everything we lean on in order to survive doesn't work for us. We try to use our mind to think positively, but the number of issues thrown at us begins to cut us instead of bouncing off. Imagine knocking on a brick wall with your knuckles with a light level of strength. The first few times will probably not affect your knuckles but keep going in the same force and timing. Keep knocking. What would happen? After a little while, you'll feel pain, frustration, and then cuts, bleeding, and eventually you'd stop because the pain is unbearable, and the outcome will be a badly cut and bruised hand that will need attention to heal and recover. The feeling of overwhelm, can feel the same, without having to ram your knuckles into a wall.

We go through emotional stress. This, again, is intangible. It's the energy we have that causes us to feel anxiety, fear, nervousness, and our body's reaction, can have a natural tendency to either fight or fly. In times where we're given a multitude of tasks to accomplish but can feel enormous pressure recognizing that time isn't on our side at all. In my case, I was overwhelmed by the poor relationships in my life.

The first man I loved in my life, my dad, abandoned me emotionally and had been hard on me ever since that one Saturday night he slammed the door in my face. He left with my mom to another state and barely stayed in touch with me, resenting me for not following him, and all his actions had affected my mother so negatively that she called me every day in deep tears and loneliness for being his wife and feeling trapped in a world she never imagined she would be in.

The next man who told me he'd love me forever, couldn't. He worried so much that he'd prefer cheating than believing in us. The next man wanted forever with me, but secretly never left his girlfriend. And the next man, was determined to keep me in his life so he could manipulate, control, and break me.

My friends in college were busy being in college and making new friends in a new town where we were isolated and discriminated in the gated community we were in, was just a depressing scene itself. And between all that shit and my father's incessant need to blame me for my injuries, to make fun of me because I lost partial hearing, and to convince me that I'm not ever going to be good enough for anyone, I was in a blurred state of mind. I felt so pressured and broken emotionally that I didn't know what was right or wrong anymore when it came to me.

I lost most of the love I had left in myself. I was more ashamed, embarrassed, and emotionally lifeless. It felt as if no matter what I did, no matter what I said, I was abused physically and emotionally for two decades from people whom I loved and respected. My mind, heart, and spirit were spinning out of control. I started to wonder if the purpose I had in this life was to be everyone's piñata: show up to the event, just to be beaten down.

I remember my final attempt to escape the guy who had an abusive control over me. I was alone, crying, and fell to my knees. In moments of full-blown overwhelm, the hidden power I had rested within my silence. In the darkness. Through my quiet tears.

The silence allowed me to focus on the moment I was in. To listen to me. Staying silent allowed me to hear myself, my pain, and what my inner dialog was saying. I heard myself sad, miserable, and afraid. I hated who I was with, hated how he made me feel and hated seeing myself feeling stuck, and not knowing what I can do to leave successfully. When I tuned in to the dialog in my mind, it gave me the chance to take notice and decide if I wanted to continue hearing this painful inner-conversation for the rest of my life.

Do we ever really listen to what *we* say to ourselves? Or are we hanging on to the opinions of others for us to believe in ourselves? I mean, did I want to sound this sad forever? Didn't I deserve to feel better?

In the silence, the weak side of me was so angry and upset at the life I was in and how diminished I felt. Whatever durable power of me was left told me enough was enough.

It led me to the other power that, no matter how many ways I had seen this done on the surface of my existence in churches, temples, and synagogues, I didn't know it would impact me when I meant it. It became the ultimate power that had always been available. I just had to fully surrender to it: The power of prayer.

Suicide

Suicide is such a visceral word. I never imagined that word would ever enter my mind. I never really used that word; I just chose the idea of leaving. I want to take you to that place I was in so it can be better understood. No matter how the exterior and environment looked, no matter how much I smiled and laughed. No matter how much I loved with all my heart, and how much I respected everyone I could, I constantly heard what I translated to being their disproval of my existence.

It wasn't about me not liking who I was. It was more about being convinced by my environment that my definition of myself was wrong. When you're in an environment that feels like an emotional pressure cooker, your mind deteriorates, and your heart feels like it's going to explode.

I thought I was a good kid, a fun friend, a loving, trusting, and loyal person. But with everything I heard and everything I saw done to me by people who said they loved me – I didn't like the love story I was in. It felt like no matter how hard I worked for others I was discredited, disproved, and dismissed. No one wanted to make wrongs right. No one wanted to work anything out. If they messed up, I could forgive them, but if I messed up, I was emotionally exiled and physically abandoned.

After I prayed in my condo for help, it was the next day when circumstances led me to have the strength to end all ties with my abuser. A few days went by, and while I was at work on the phone as a telemarketer for a sunroom company, he had gotten the operator to cut into my call to talk with me. He broke into my home, and he wasn't leaving until I worked things out. He was so sorry. He wanted to make all wrongs right. He didn't want it to be over. He wanted me to be his wife.

I didn't call the police. I didn't have the voice of reason to tell me the better option. I just wanted to end this amicably. I'll go home and talk to him, and he'll leave.

I woke up in the hospital the next day. I opened my eyes and saw my parents at the end of my hospital bed. My head was wrapped, sling around my left shoulder and arm, and my emotions were annihilated. I had nothing left except my sight, seeing a blurred vision of my parents. I closed my eyes and asked God to take me. I was done.

I saw myself fully committed to kindness, listening, loving, and doing all the things that I was supposed to do for family, friends, and significant others. I followed what everyone wanted of me, but the outcome never felt like an accomplishment. I never felt my worth.

I fell into an abusive relationship with a guy who isolated me from everyone so he could have full control over me. I even tried to be strong enough to leave, but the only way I could, according to him, was over my dead body.

I didn't have a problem believing I was worthy, but the conversations, abandonment and constant fights for getting something right back in my life kept telling me that I wasn't enough for any of them. I either couldn't rise to their standards, so they'd leave or betray me, or they'd tell me that they can't rise to my standards because I wanted was a reciprocation of effort. And now, in a hospital, broken, abused, torn, all after trying to prove to my father that I didn't need to be controlled by him, and trying to create a life so I can bring my mom back to fulfill the plan I've had for most of my life: bringing her back to the happiness she so deserved – seeing where I was, I just wanted to let go.

I couldn't fight the battles anymore. I faced the reality that I wouldn't win the war. I didn't want to prove I was worth anything to anyone. I didn't want to hear anyone tell me I wasn't good enough for anything I aspired to become.

My emotional energy was raped. My belief in myself was tortured. My worth – what worth? All I had was taken from me.

I saw spoiled brats being loved and forgiven. I saw ruthless shitty people have family who stuck by their side, even when they're wrong. Especially when they're wrong.

When I was mildly wrong, I got beat with whatever was available. When a friend manipulated something I did, friends preferred to side with the manipulator, instead of the truth. And, in general, it felt like the simple act of being me was a bad idea in the eyes of people who were supposed to support and grow me. I was a flower in everyone else's storm, and I hated being in that storm for two decades.

My name wasn't Job from the Bible. It was Anita, the scrawny, foolish, waste of a child, black sheep in the family. The stupid Hindu. The soul who wasn't good enough to love back, but good enough to take advantage of over and over, daily, yearly, per decade.

May 13. Third day in the hospital. I faintly heard the nurses wish me a happy birthday. Nothing like celebrating the day you were born at a time where all you want to do is die so you wouldn't be a burden to anyone anymore.

They wished me a happy birthday, but I couldn't hear them. I lost my hearing in both ears. Funny, how that worked out. Symbolic, actually. I didn't want to hear from anyone anymore. I didn't want sympathy. I didn't want anyone to do anything for me.

No attending my funeral. No paying respect.

I take issue with people who suddenly show up after someone passes who never righted wrongs. I think it's a heavy tragedy to go to a funeral to "pay respect" if you spent your time with the person disrespecting them while they were alive, and never made things right. I can't see the point in waiting until someone dies to finally pay respect. Wouldn't you want to respect them while you have them alive and, in your life, to enjoy? But droves of people show up when people die. Swarms of followers suddenly pay tribute to important people and their contribution, after they're dead. I didn't get this world. I thought we were supposed to love and respect through the challenges, not love and respect after they're gone. I can understand seeing people who have invested the time coming to grieve, who may not be as tight of a connection as others. I get that. I don't get that person or family who suddenly flies in from Mars to pay respect. That "better late than never" phrase doesn't work here, sorry. Time's up.

I was checked out emotionally. I saw myself taken from my hometown in a wheelchair, after having all my personal belongings secretly viewed and either given away or destroyed without my knowledge. I flew to my parents' new home.

A part of me was feeling below the surface of painfully unworthy, embarrassed, and unhappy. I was tired of smiling through the bullshit. I was done holding my tongue when people drenched me with insults, criticisms, and ugly words.

I felt like I was on a ship filled with the community of people I cared about, but they'd collaborate to throw me into an ocean. And every time I'd swim back to the ship and climb back up. Over and over and over again. Each time frustrating and wondering why they're throwing me away.

And each time I was thrown I was losing my strength in swimming back. It was getting harder after a decade. And I found myself not wanting to swim back to the ship anymore. I got the picture. They didn't want me. I got it. I just hated that I didn't agree with their decision. But there was no other ship to swim to and I was losing the strength to tread water. I wanted to let go.

I went into the shower one morning when I woke up in my parents' home. I could hear my parents talking downstairs. Bickering. My mom emotional about how my dad is talking about me causing this to happen. My mom standing up for me. Ugh. I felt so horrible for her having to constantly fight for herself and for me. He's driven her crazy and whatever fight she has left in her for the greater good, she is using it on him. I hated the scene and I felt worse that I was only adding to her troubles. The liability in his life is ruining their marriage. She can't leave him. I can't take her away because I'm stuck in this emotional prison again.

I felt so overwhelmed with the guilt of burdening my parents, family and friends. My life couldn't just be peaceful and normal like so many lives I'd seen. I was so tired of the men in my life who told me they loved me when they weren't down with upholding the meaning of the word love. Their definition was different than mine.

As strong as I had acted and appeared on the outside, I was ripped to shreds emotionally on the inside. Imagine the most grotesque scene where someone was horribly tortured, brutally beaten, bones shattered, skin ripped and on her last breath. Now amp it up to a heinous level times 100, and that may just be the appearance of how things looked on the emotional side of my existence. Holding on. One bated breath at a time.

As I stood in the shower and looked at the water falling on my face, I suddenly felt a surge of sadness crash out from my eyes, and I began to bawl. I covered my mouth to keep my pain muted. It wasn't the ugly cry. It was far worse. It came from an incredibly dark and buried place – I'd suspect it was my soul's sadness.

I didn't want my parents to hear. I didn't want them to feel burdened with another problem from their worthless child. I just wrapped myself up in my towel and cried into another towel as I sat on my bed and looked out the window that was about ten feet away from me.
That window. It looked so fantastic.

It felt like it was the only way out.

My exit strategy.

If I left, no one would have to make fun of me. No one would have to find fault with me. No one would have to feel like I was a liability. I could leave, and they can all feel relief from the release of such a useless waste of time and space. Yes. This feels like a perfect solution.

I became 99% convinced that they were right about me. All those comments that echoed in my mind. Reminders of being unwanted. I felt like I was under a spell as I looked at the window. My mind became so keen to believe that if I ran as fast as I could right out that window, it would hurt for just a little bit, but

- the pain of my father being stuck with a useless daughter like me would be gone

- the worry my mom has of me having to deal with my narcissistic father would be over

- my friends have plenty of friends that matter more, so no loss there

- the loves of my life are already loving someone else, no fuss no muss.

I asked God to take me when I was in the hospital, and even He didn't think I was worth to bring back Home. That's okay. I got this. It's the only way. I was 99% convinced.

But that 1%...

Chapter Fifteen: My Pause
Playlist: Fix You – Coldplay

That one percent.

99% of me was ready to race through that window that was calling to me. It felt like the best answer to all the burden I thought I was causing.

But that one percent – it was made up of two actions:

1. a Divine request
2. a human response

0.5% was a Divine request I heard through my heart:

"Wait…"

I was asked to pause. UGH. 99% of me was ready to go, full speed. Heart racing. Mind exploding. Spirit falling.

"Wait…"

I felt a strong pull to hold me down. To keep me seated.

0.5% was my effort to respond. To pause. To wait. Five-tenths of my power graced the Divine request by pressing pause on my internal remote control that was playing out the life I was ready to end.

That 0.5% became everything to me.

For most of my life, my faith was based on following what my mom told me to do:

Put your hands together like this and pray.
Don't worry about what you're saying. Just pray.
My mother taught me, and now I'm teaching you.
We're singing praise to God.
Don't worry about why. Just do.

And hearing my father's words about my mom's way of believing:

You're bribing God.
You're making vows.
There's nothing after you die.
All this you're doing is for nothing.
Don't bother asking why.
It's just a show you're giving.
God won't answer you.
You're praying to God?
What God...
You're just a fool.

While we followed the tradition of doing things because our generations told us to, I never really appreciated traditional practices.

If I didn't have an explanation to offer a reason, the don't-ask-anyone-questions-just-do-it approach didn't appeal to me. But I always had a relationship with the Almighty. I always felt something special between Him and me. I can't explain it, but I still talk to Him from my heart.

My energy felt a certain passion that wasn't created by me but instead swirled within me. I understood the profound meaning of "Namaste," where one pays respect to the energy of God residing within the other. I understood what *Swami Vivekananda* said in his book *Lectures from Colombo to Almora* published in 1897:

"Stand up and express the divinity within you."

This message was so profound and said so long ago. And I'm sure the words across time have been there from all the great messengers representing The Almighty. All the greats across the globe have shared messages that lead to loving who you are, where you came from, that you are here for a great purpose and always remembering that you're loved.

You just have to believe it.

When I had no one to talk to (which was more often than you'd imagine), I spoke to the Almighty. And I'd feel the response over time.

But there was a time from my teens thru my 20s where the ease to go wayward increased substantially when distractions of desire, ugliness, and control continuously constricted me from myself. There was only one time where I fell to my knees amid a horrible relationship asking the Almighty in every name, I could imagine that represented Him.

It was my 0.5% contribution toward Him, when I gave 99.5% to everyone else. Terrible, as I look back. I was, in essence, the Bible's Prodigal Child.

My whole body felt cold when I had this uncontrollable desire to bolt through that fantastic window, but when I felt the Divine message of "Wait…" it halted everything. In my pause, I took my first deep breath and did what was asked, still looking at that window, eyes still wet with tears. My body suddenly thawed with warmth.

The moment made me nervous. I had no idea what the hell was going on, but all the goosebumps vanished, and I felt warm from the inside out. I slowly turned away from the window and unintentionally looked at the wall in front of me between two closets. A small lighted image was glowing on the wall that I thought for sure was made from the windows' design behind me.

I turned back to the windows to myth-bust the gasp I had at what I saw on that wall. The light that was cast from the windows didn't match the pattern on the wall.

I gasped again. I looked back at the window, and then again at the image on the wall. It was a small pattern. I opened and closed my eyes repeatedly, thinking y eyes aren't focused right. I wiped my tears to make sure I wasn't losing my shit.

Nope. It was still there.

The image of the pattern I thought was on the wall, wasn't on the wall. I grabbed my heart. Tears flooded out of my eyes. I looked around and realized that the image that I saw on the wall was actually an image that was coming out of my eyes, projecting on the wall.

The light was in my eyes.

I know. Impossible. Insanity. Delusional. No scientific explanation so chalk me up as a nut job. That's fine. I don't care. I'm not even the slightest bit concerned about convincing a soul.

The moment was mine and just like the millions of people who have near-death experiences, miracles and other incredible moments, I guess I'll say that *that* was the most touching, shocking, fantastic moment I'd ever had in my life, and it came to me just a microsecond before I was about to end it.

Wrapped in warmth, I played with this image in my eyes for a moment, because I couldn't believe this was happening. I looked up, down, around – to see if this image would leave – but it didn't. At this point you're wondering what in the world was this image coming out from my eyes onto the wall?

The image of light that was in my eyes was that of the Holy Cross.

This glowing Cross glowed in my eyes strong enough that I could see it everywhere I looked. It stayed in my eyes for I can't recall how long, but long enough for me to change into my clothes and make the decisions I needed to make to bring me to where I am today.

His 0.5% toward me was nothing less than amazing. The warm spiritual "hug" washed over my desire to unburden my family, friends, and anyone who found fault with my existence. In His great way, He told me that I mattered to Him, and that – to me – became more than enough. I never really knew He cared like that.

I learned from everyone else to fear God. To do as your told and follow the rules "...or you'll dieeeeeee!" With so many e's, like I would die so badly because I didn't follow the exact rules.

Fire and brimstone.
Hell.
Devil's gonna get me.
Oooooooooo...

All that fear thrown from so many angles. Fear in my life never came from the Almighty, it came from humans. That Cross was the representation of Him telling me that while no one seemed to be there for me, He was. My hearing was removed for a short amount of time, and in its place, He filled my eyes with an image I recognized that said, "But I still love you..."

It was the only most profound experience I had ever had that took place because I gave Him 0.5% of me.

I believe in all my heart that the Almighty will find His way to speak to us and will provide whatever means He can that can identify with who we are and what would work for us. And I believe He does show His reminders as love notes to us daily, even multiple times if we tune in to that station. That's His contribution. It's up to us to provide our part of the deal into recognizing it, embracing it, and taking action with the powers He's given us. If we can identify the little love notes that are hidden in our daily living, we might recognize just how much we're loved.

Even if no one else can see you, I can say with all my heart, He can.

He thinks you're more than enough. He should know. He created you. And because He created you, He provided you with incredible intangible powers to see, hear, taste, think, do, remember, feel, wait, and believe.

He also blessed you with a body as your most excellent tangible tool of all tools to help you use your intangible powers for the greater good.

The Almighty became the apex of all superheroes in my world. The His cape graces the entire multiverse of existence! So, if He is who He is, and He created who we are, filled with intangible powers within our human construct, well, that makes us Undercover Superheroes.

Just like Clark Kent became Superman, and Diana Prince became Wonder Woman, you can become mightier than you believe you are today when you recognize who you are, what powers you have, and are ready to rock and roll. This is your time to step out of the shadows that others cast upon you, and into the light that was always within you.

Chapter Sixteen: My Tribe
Playlist: You Gotta Be – Des 'Ree

For so long, it always felt like an "us vs. them" experience for me.

"Us" represented the better and accepting society. They were the other Indian people in my life who knew their native language and chose to use it in front of me, without translation, even if they knew how to speak English well.

The non-Indian friends who found their culture fascinating and mine weird, because it wasn't theirs.

The manager who yelled at me daily, wrote me up as often as he could and treated me so poorly, with his only reason being that I "was Indian."

The light-skinned Indians who looked at me wondering where from India could I have possibly come from because I didn't fit the stereotype. The dark-skinned Indians who felt the same. The modeling industry that told me that I could only pass for the Hispanic market because "there's no market for Indian people."

"Them" represented the outcasts, wallflowers, pariahs, and misfits. That's my tribe.

I saw the famous "Crazy Ones" quote from the 1997 "Think Different" Campaign by Apple, Inc. written by Rob Siltanen and his creative team for Apple in my 20's:

"Here's to the crazy ones. The misfits. The rebels. The troublemakers. The round pegs in the square holes. The ones who see things differently. They're not fond of rules. And they have no respect for the status quo. You can quote them, disagree with them, glorify or vilify them. About the only thing you can't do is ignore them. Because they change things. They push the human race forward. And while some may see them as the crazy ones, we see genius. Because the people who are crazy enough to think they can change the world are the ones, who do."

"The crazy ones. The misfits. The ones who see things differently." I identified with those words deeply in my heart. It was not only a grand message from Apple, Inc., a socially accepted and successful company that told everyone who wasn't a part of the "crazy ones" tribe that it's time to start appreciating them; it was an even mightier message that inspired me to recognize the power within me that I buried away for another day.

The message told me what I believed already, but hearing it in the way it was said, at the time I needed to listen to it, was a huge high five that practically gave me the go-ahead nod to be okay with being me. That I wasn't alone. That I had the power to make change happen, and not to conform to any standard that others pushed me toward. That was precisely what I tried to do all of my life: I worked my round-pegged self through every square hole and suffered the consequences.

Superman would have been seen as a misfit. A nerd. A weirdo. A strange dude. But he showed us through the comics and silver screen that his power was designed with the purpose to not only benefit you but benefit others, too. And that the greater good was not limited to the fantasies on the silver screen and paper. That they were conduits to encourage and influence us to help do the same for others as well.

It opened my mind to recognizing a critical thought about Undercover Superheroes: we aren't humans pretending to be superheroes; we are humans recognizing the superheroes within us.

If you're a superhero fan like I am, take a moment and think about what you love most about your favorite superhero. Most likely, you'll identify traits and strengths that might match your talents and passions. I asked my husband who his favorite superhero was. He told me the superhero Flash. I asked him what it was about Flash that makes him the favorite. He said, "His speed." When my husband looked back on his school years, he told me he was the fastest sprinter and hurdler, as well as the highest and farthest jumper on two track teams.

What we love about superheroes is most often what we already have within ourselves. We're so busy recognizing and admiring the awesomeness of the superheroes out there, that we don't notice the similar traits and powers we also have within us. Our own powers are what gravitate us to identifying and admiring that superhero.

I asked different people who were fans of a particular superhero what they specifically loved about that selection. What was it about that superhero that they loved the most? Each person answered a quality that either they also had, or that amplified a passion that they were already drawn to. As each person would talk through their love of the superhero they focused on, they began seeing the similarities, almost like they recognized that they were nearly cut from the same cloth. The moment that connection happened, some eyes grew and sparkled with a surprise that they had anything like the superhero did. They sat up taller, began to smile wider, feeling happily surprised. Some stifled or squelched the idea, because they couldn't imagine they could be that impactful, or taking literal translation like saying, "well I can't be Wonder Woman, because I don't have an invisible jet."

I saw a quote that graced my eyes as I was researching for some information. It was an authorless quote in how I saw it, but I wish I could credit whoever wrote it because it hit the feeling I've felt in the past twenty-plus years that I've been working with people:

"We're all superheroes pretending to be ordinary people."

I loved that message. I loved it so much because it almost spells out the struggle that people go through with that action word "pretending." I remember the number of kids, including myself pretending to be a superhero: We'd dress up, style our hair (or in my case throw it in a bun) and commit to the overt physical actions that we see portrayed on the screen to emulate the power of that superhero.

We had our appreciation right in focusing on the awesomeness of the superheroes, but we might not have paid closer attention to their emotional strength and behavior that keeps them getting back up, to their focus power dedicated to achieving their missions, to their will to endure the pain, frustration, and challenges that come their way, or to their temper (except for The Incredible Hulk), in how they handle the pushback or setback – how they reach for resources to aid them where they need.

We act as if we're humans pretending to be superheroes. What if we just switched that up? What if we believed we are superheroes pretending to be human? That, in my belief, would make so much more sense, seeing the unlimited potential unlocked, unleashed, revealed and embraced by millions already. The powers we need are already within us. We were given strengths and talents but miss out on the necessary training to improve what we were given so we can use what we have for the greater good.

Pay more attention to the stories of the superheroes. When *DC Comics* and *Marvel's* Clark Kent, Bruce Wayne, Tony Stark, Diana Prince, and Carol Danvers discover what they have, they focus and train hard and continuously, until they become a master of it, and then use it to master their universe, which would be their emotional, intellectual and physical world. We were designed with powers specific to us. When we spend less time focused on what's out there to connect and more time looking within to engage and grow, I wholeheartedly believe your Undercover Superhero will step right into the light within you, and shine. Take time to look within and learn about what you're made of.

What are your default powers? What is your superpower? Now, imagine everyone who lacks the power you have.

People who need you to

- help them out of their situation,
- teach them how to accomplish something,
- inspire them to keep on moving,
- redirect them toward the path of least resistance,
- aim to adjust and improve for the greater good, and
- encourage them to reveal and preserve their truth as Undercover Superheroes.

You, my friend, have an Undercover Superhero beaming within you. You're here for a purpose, just like I was, and I never really knew it. I almost died twice to realize it. You don't have to get to that point to reach for your illumination.

Chapter Seventeen: My Mind Power
Playlist: Best of You – Foo Fighters

Mission: Harness your mind power.

At 39 years old, *Maya Angelou* looked me in the eyes and eloquently, emotionally spoke about how important it is to be careful in the words we use or permit in our house. I listened; my breath hinged on her every word. I heard her. But at that moment, she wasn't talking to me; she was speaking for me.

I listened to her words, escorted by her nurturing and thoughtful voice. *Oprah's* television show *Master Class*, continued that hour with her educating the viewers about life, experiences, the importance of who we are, and most importantly, the power in the choice of words we use.

After the show ended, I meditated about what *Ms. Angelou* said. Words were very powerful for me through my life and are used so poorly by too many people to hurt, discount, dismiss or bully/control. Words are the messengers for our feelings, the tone being something like the customer service in the delivery of the message.

I believe, what goes neglected is the power of the home that we genuinely don't reside in enough: our heart. Society has us looking at the heart and equating it to love. While I'm also someone who has followed that thought, placing my hand to my heart in the allegiance I have to my American flag or when moments touch me ("touches my heart"), the reality is that love resides in our mind, along with all the other emotions.

It's like one big inner-family. But that inner-family of emotions becomes dysfunctional when we allow certain members of the family take over. When we permit other people's feelings to suffocate our own; when we become an emotional martyr, sacrificing crucial moments that could have allowed us to grow, we contribute to the problem. We enable, which contributes to building on an already negative situation, because giving permission to a poor behavior can often say "it's okay to do that to me" when it's completely not okay.

Sometimes, these situations get so bad, that when we give so much of ourselves to a bad deal, we risk becoming one of the worst abusers to ourselves, than the people we gave the abusing credit to.

Yep, I said that. I held myself responsible once I began to learn better, to know better, and try for better. I know that we're not all given the situations to stand on a soapbox and let our feelings out, expecting our world to join in our chant. I'm not recommending you do that, either. What I'm saying is that we have work to do in knowing what intangible powers we were given, understanding how each power works efficiently and what it takes for those powers to work for us at optimum level.

When is it the right time to use specific powers? How much of it do we dispense? What forces are best left in our power vault? For example - people who cook, who are chefs in their kitchen, imagine this:

A spoon, a butter knife, a melon baller, a butcher's knife, and a serrated knife.

If I told you I had a chuck roast, crusty Italian bread, cream cheese, ½ an avocado and ½ of a watermelon, you've probably already naturally paired which food item would go with the tool.

If I told you that I cut my roast into cubes with a butter knife, used a melon baller to cut a slice of the crusty Italian bread, the Butcher's knife to spread cream cheese onto a bagel, the serrated knife to scoop the full avocado out from its skin, and a spoon to cut slices of watermelon for a picnic, the average cook in the kitchen would think I'm nuts. The daredevils that want to win some *Food Network* competition would say that somehow in some way, it's possible, but even if it could be accomplished, it will be annoying, frustrating, and in the end, probably have a mess to clean up. My point? We use our tools to create the best outcome for what we want out of life. Looking to create a mess? Well, now you know what to do. Use your essential tools in the wrong way and your mess will show up. Ignore it long enough and your messes will take over, and you'll be stuck with a lot of clean up in the end.

The image I share gives a quick-and-easy reference to three reminders we should train our brain to default to when we think of mind power:

Reminder 1: The Universe

If life were television, then we should know more about the Universal Broadcast System that comes equipped with one all-time amazing cable station called The UCS (the Untouchable Cable Station). This cable station comes with three incredible channels that we all have access to - no installation necessary!

1. Al Mighty
2. Mr. Experience &
3. Mrs. Time.

Without them, I wouldn't be who I am today.

A. **"Al Mighty"** is precisely who you think it is, and the most crucial channel that I'll take a little extra time sharing the *why* here. Al is The One. The Force. A fun play on words, yes, but also created to reposition the great omniscient, omnipotent and omnipresent respectfully to our casual level of understanding, because there are too many people out there who speak more complicated than I do.

I believe there are quintuple the number of people who could appreciate a more casual conversation about AI so they can reconnect with a little more ease. I've heard that many live a God-fearing life, but I haven't focused on fear with AI Mighty. I have always focused on a *God-respecting* default in my behavior and reciprocation for my life experiences. I wholeheartedly respect His existence and honestly believe, that if He has anger, it's well-deserved.

Humans, in general, kind of suck in listening skills. I say that with love. I mean, from Adam and Eve not listening to direct instructions, to Aaron and his crew giving up on Moses and creating the golden calf from their gold belongings, to the big New Testament moment in John 18:40 where the community all collectively asked to spare the criminal and murderer, Barabbas, and instead crucify Jesus.

The compassion of God to go through lifetimes watching His children disrespect, neglect, change their mind, fight and hurt as much as they do – and still love, has got to be beyond any level I can put into words. Of course, He holds power to end everything at any time He wishes.

He instead has us figuring things out for ourselves, which often is the better approach when we think of authoritative parenting. He is the ultimate parent. If you're the kind of kid who refuses to listen, holds barely any self-control and continues to make the same mistakes over and over again, I guess I, too, would live in full-blown anxiety over the kind of trouble we might get into once we get back Home. My point here is to tune in more often to His love channel and look for the moments that share how much love He has for us. How much He forgives. And all the messages, nudges, and "coincidental" ways He enters our journey to say, "I love you."

Al is my BFF, my favorite relative, my everlasting father and mother, my twin sibling, my teacher, my guide, my instructor, my voice of reason, and beyond a shadow of a doubt, my ultimate perfect life coach. Al has always been around, nudging us, setting our alarms to go off, warning us, blessing us, forgiving us and providing powers to us as we develop from infancy to where we are today – and eventually through who we will become, as life unfolds down our path.

We're given this incredibly powerful channel within us to purge our toxic thoughts, feelings, and burdens that are too great for us. We're to switch to this channel to also plugin, as it is the supercharger of all-electric chargers you'll ever find in your existence. You have to plug in, and you'll feel the surge. When you're out and about, taking care of your daily missions, He stays in contact with you through moments and messages that we all gauge as "signs," coincidences, the interesting happening, the strange moment, the gut-feeling (which I prefer to call it God-Feeling), and intuition.

Most people who are in abusive situations and relationships, might start off saying they never saw it coming, but if we dig a little deeper, AI was flagging us all down. First as a whisper, then a nudge, then a shove, then a throw and finally a slam before He lets you do you, whatever that is. He tries for you for a long time. If you're a parent or guardian of any child who suffers you might have understood that feeling where you talk kindly first, then you're more assertive, then aggressive, then you're hardcore, then after the madness and yelling and slamming to exclaim how much you want your kid to straighten out before anything worse can happen, even if you know you'll never give up on him or her, you have to let go.

In that feeling of letting go, if you feel what I'm talking about, you might relate a smidge to what AI deals with daily with the entire planet, at the least. AI is so mighty that he not only supplies the power of alert and warning, but He lights us up with positive emotional, logical, and spiritual thoughts and feelings.

We get that "it feels right" feeling. Ever have a moment when you're lost driving, and without the GPS or map, you paused for a moment, and then choose a turn that felt like it was the correct decision, and it was? When you get conscious about the powers you're given and born with, you'll not only feel pretty amazing; you'll replace fears with confidence in your missions. You'll know what to do and what tool to use when necessary. Al Mighty is the all-time best channel I have ever switched to, and I tend to be on that channel at least two to three times a day, if not more. Staying engaged in that program reaps super heroic benefits for successful outcomes from the inside out.

B. **Mr. Experience** is the channel that not only engages you with possibilities in enriching your talents and offering you new opportunities to explore your unlimited potential, it also provides you a treasure of an incredibly added benefit called memory. You can look back and recall your history of not only trials and errors, setbacks, frustrations, and losses, you also get to look back at the positive moments. The joy, happiness, success, achievements, equations that worked, and the power you had to survive and thrive through it. You made all of that goodness happen by the power of your existence, despite all the odds.

Mr. Experience is the most exceptional strength trainer to help you build authority, endurance, and flexibility within your mental, emotional and spiritual muscle. Get your reps and sets in daily!

C. **Mrs. Time** is such an incredibly powerful channel, and unfortunately, she's too often neglected or taken for granted. It's probably because she asks for patience, management, and focus, three areas that most of the human population suffer from in terms of excellence. This channel has a way of making us feel extreme angst like toddlers in the back-seat exclaiming, "are we there yet??!!" where moments feel like forever. It can also have us feeling shocked that the moment has arrived already like parents seeing their child get their driver's license or reaching high school or college graduation. Surprised where the time went and amazed at how fast it flew by.

I remember hearing my husband's grandmother share four wise words, when hard moments invaded happy hearts: *This too shall pass*. I know plenty of people who want to choke those four words because they need change to happen now. Yesterday. Last year. And they have to do the thing that they don't want to do: Wait.

When time is of the essence, waiting is torture. Just watch video footage of the Chicago Board of Trade or the old Mercantile Exchange (CME) pit traders back in the '80s and '90s to see how intensely each second of time was used to achieve a serious financial gain.

Commerce is dependent upon emotionally inspired purchases, first impressions, and instant appreciation that leads to trending sales to reach maximum growth.

Imagine Mrs. Time as the bookkeeper for your life's mental, emotional and spiritual investments and expenses, she's also your holistic doctor and the patient grandmother who knows what's beneath the surface of that emotional iceberg you're keeping under wraps. Remember the 0.5% effort mentioned in Chapter 15? Had I not made a choice to give that request the attention it asked. If I didn't wait, I know I wouldn't have been here. I wouldn't have moved back to Chicago, made the friendships I made, experienced the adventures I had, worked the jobs I did, married the man I still love, have the daughter I adore and create the opportunities I've created to bring positive influences, experiences, and inspiration to those who needed it.

I spent my life having a plan. I had one for my mom. I came so close to reaching that, but time ran out, and I lost her to Alzheimer's. She was 77 years old. Diagnosed in '96. My father left America, and sent her away to live in India, until he could close shop and join her. And, well, the stories from there will have to wait until the right time.

Losing her memory may have been a blessing more than a curse, because the only memory she kept with her 'til her last days was of me. I made a vow that I would do what I could to help others keep the kind of relationship my mother had from happening to anyone. She was in a very emotionally abusive relationship that was so hard on her, Al Mighty brought her back on August 15, 2005. That date is Independence Day in India. Poetically perfect.

When we can respect the value Mrs. Time brings to us, we'll come not only to appreciate the time that's given to us, but we'll also make a conscious effort in managing our time with quality and respectful experiences as our moments become memories.

Reminder 2: The Triangle

Of all the shapes we're given, the triangle is the best shape of all geometric shapes in the math and physics world.

I've learned over the years that the triangle is the most fundamental selection used in constructing physical and virtual realities. It is the strongest of all shapes, where when a force is placed on a triangle, the energy is spread to all three sides. Triangles are also the most rigid and stable of all shapes. All other polygons are not rigid like the triangle.

In the spiritual realm, a triangle pointing upward is a representation of positive power. Delta is a Greek symbol Δ that denotes change and is used in math, physics, engineering, and now here to help you view this fantastic, powerful shape to represent your powers in:

- exceptional strength that you do have within your mind: logic and emotion combined

- balance/stability, to help you stay rigid in your values, actions and balance well through the juggling game life plays with you

- delta, the whole shape itself speaks a strong message: embrace and observe the power of change that you have within you.

Reminder 3: The Controls

 I opted to provide images within the powerful triangle that every person who ever owned a television with a remote control could easily understand:

- At the top is the universal symbol for power itself, and your influence to turn that power on within you.

- To the left is the symbol for pause, an often-under-rated action. Press pause for as little as a microsecond. Listen. Rest/relax. Observe. Wait. It has the power to change everything if you use it or choose to never pause and change nothing.

- To the right, the symbol for play. Literally and figuratively, in every way you're able to, choose to play. Keep your life and thinking fun, playful and enjoy your ride.

Everyone is looking for the fountain of youth outside of themselves when all the while, it resides within your head through your ever-loving mind. Press play as often as you can to keep joy as the true fire in your spirit.

We can get caught up in the mundane routines, or deal with aggravating people and happenings or get knee-deep in downright messed-up situations that take hold of our emotions. We could stay there and claim SNAFU (situation normal, all fucked up) throw all issues in a Vitamix blender and turn it all into a terrible smoothie not worth digesting. We can easily do that. It's most likely what a lot of people are doing now with something in their life.

How about instead of that route, we now do a little more work enriching the power we have within ourselves that'll propel us to become stronger and freer from other people's emotional and intellectual storms?

There's an incredibly valuable feeling humans strive for, called *worth*. Without it we fall prey to desperation, anger, resentment, rebellion, confusion and frustration.

Some people mask their insecurities with excessive doses of ego. A healthy ego's purpose is to protect your sense of security and survival, not to invade, occupy, annihilate, and destroy. That's an abuse of a usually fantastic power.

The ego takes the driver's seat and leads the way with abandon. While our ego drives, the source for a reason hides behind the ego's Power of Attorney position and is all too often overlooked. If you recognize any of these shortcomings, it's time to come to terms with seizing your power back.

From A Weakening to An Awakening

I defined myself early in life based on the opinions, practices, and criticisms of the people in my environment. I only knew that their job description for me was to get them and keep them proud of me, but the emotional obstacle courses they built made the *American Ninja Warrior* competition look like a kid's hopscotch pattern on a playground.

I took the verbal punches, accepted neglect, smiled reluctantly, and kept sad feelings on the inside. Compliments, encouragement, and support weren't values in my childhood. Respect was, but not for me, just for everyone else. Most classmates, friends, and community never knew the underbelly of my tapestry. I chose to show them the finished picture that I envisioned instead of the knotted, tangled yarn that represented my home and heart life.

For them, I made it a point to be a joyful, fun person who stayed involved in a lot of school activities. But for me, I was struggling under the radar. While I was determined to gain my sense of worth, while having it recognized and appreciated, I was given more experiences that fought me to the ground to prove me otherwise. This ugly mental and emotional tug of war built my insecurity, and I worked my ass off to take that beast out. No vacancy.

Five Emotional Self-Defense Strategies to Overcome Insecurity

In the '70s, we had a limited number of shows we could watch before we heard the National Anthem, saw our flag wave and then static/dead air, so I enjoyed watching the shows that made it to television. I spent most of my childhood watching T.V., so I'm relating my following points in that theme.

When you watch a show, and it either doesn't cater to your interest, or it shares information that doesn't suit you, what do you do? Well, back the day, maybe you or your parents would get up and change the channel. You tuned in to a channel that was something more of your style and interest.

Later, the television world received more shows, 24-hour coverage, and the remote control. What's the most common thing we either did, said, or was told for to us to do when it comes to the remote control? "Change the channel!" That's your first of five Emotional Self-Defense Strategies (ESDS).

Recognize that as well as the remaining four strategies, and you're golden.

ESDS1. Change the Channel. When it comes to the insecurities developed from my upbringing, I had to create a habit that would enrich my happiness instead of reducing it. I'd change the channel in my mind, when the shows in front of my life's screen didn't suit me.

ESDS2. Press Pause. When I say pause, I mean, I took a passionate pause. As I watched experiences play out that could affect me, pressing pause helped me focus on observation, learning more and gives me the time to make smarter decisions instead of hasty reacting that risked conflict. It asked me to go from being reactive to playing proactively. What are some ways I pressed pause?

- **I held my emotional response(s) back**

Bite your tongue! Count to 10! Step awaaay from the canvas! In most situations, you are not obligated to respond. You are not held at gunpoint to give the person an ounce of your energy.

If it is worth your time and you value the situation more than the relationship, then it's your decision, but if you can afford to have them wait on your reaction, go for it. Better for all parties in the end.

- **I set my expectations aside**

We often hold such strong expectations in others, and by doing that, we end up feeling really let down when they don't pull the same strength in effort as you do. You do <u>you</u>. That's how you roll. Let them either join in with you if they'd like to be where you're at or leave them happy just the way they are.

- **I slept on it**

Best action that many decision makers own. Unless it's an urgent decision, disconnect and let your mind rest and get clarity. Decide the next day or gain the information that you need to make the best choice.

- **I refocused on the intent**

What was the intention? Did the person actually intend to hurt? Did you hold intention to offend when you said what you said? Many times, people say the dumbest things. I can tell they didn't say it with intention to hurt me.

Sometimes I'd ask them to repeat that just one more time so I can be sure I heard it right, and also give them recovery opportunity. 90% of the time recovery takes place. 10% has me reposition my future level of effort and involvement towards the "not so much anymore" level. They were coming from a different place of thinking, or behavior that didn't give them the memo that we just don't ask questions or say things like that. Or maybe this person is in a really bad mood and didn't really intend to do what s/he did.

ESDS3. Rewind and Replay. I never paid any respect to my accomplishments. Didn't think to take a time out to appreciate anything I'd ever really done for myself or others. I had to follow the values of others, even if I didn't agree with it. Even if it hurt. I became so consumed with trying to find out what it would take to have people in my life be happy with me and keep them from finding fault or problem, that I spent more time fighting for approval in their world than I ever appreciated anything in the world that was my own.

The negative influence that narcissistic people can have on empathic people is close to a deadly one. But I promise you, we are stronger. When we make the time to spotlight our values, we notice our worth. We need to rewind and replay so we can take the time to know all that we've done and where we've been, for us to have a personal excitement toward where we're going.

In the beginning, I wrote accomplishments in my life, from the smallest, least significant to the most substantial, most badass achievements I've ever made to protect, value, and celebrate my existence. Now, those were not the words I used in my mind as a twenty-something young lady, but it certainly was the drive and feeling.

I had to appreciate me, recognize me, celebrate me – and if no one else wanted to, at least I was going to. I owed that to myself. And you owe it to yourself to do the same. Rewind and replay.

ESDS4. DVR It: <u>D</u>o the <u>V</u>iew that's <u>R</u>ight for you. Shift your perspective from what matters to them to what matters to me. I reflect on what my Mom once told me when I was eighteen:

"The world is your canvas, and G-d provided you all the colors and brushes to paint your picture. Go and paint. Whatever you paint, it will be beautiful, because it is yours."

She was stuck in a controlling marriage, but she knew what to say to help me strengthen myself enough to never have me repeat her history.

Her words still stay with me and help me remain stable in the areas that I own. She was so right. I'd been painting everyone else's picture on my canvas, with their paint colors and brushes.

I scrapped that canvas, started over, and began a painting that would hang on my own life's wall.

Soon, when people made comments that would attempt to have me feeling less than or lack, I played a special edition of the '80s game show *Family Feud* in my head, where I'd imagine the host *Richard Dawson* with me in the final round saying,

"100 people surveyed, top answers on the board, here's the question: What is the most respectful response to 1. You're so dramatic 2. Why do you it that way? and 3. You'll never find anyone who loves you."
I'd quickly respond to each and turn around to see the points revealed per answer that would lead me to a win...

"You're so dramatic..."
Your response: I'm passionate!

Survey says!!... 25 points

"Why do you do it that way?"
Your response: Why not?

Survey says!!... 35 points, you need 40 to win Anita.

"You'll never find anyone who loves you..."
Your response: That's ok, he'll find ME.

Survey says!!... 50 points!!

[Cue *Family Feud* winning music... aaaand scene.]

ESDS5. Stop & Delete it: Take ownership back.
It's easy to get sucked into negative people's opinionated web. If we can zoom in and become more aware that their comments come from their development and design, their mentality, and their world – and not ours, we can recognize that verbal

poison and offer it the antidote within our powerful responses.

Instead of letting their negative opinions hit me, I learned to step aside and let their words hit the ground. That was a great feeling. Frequently, when someone provokes you, they're looking for a specific reaction. You know that reaction. The kind that's like "Oh yeah?? Well…" and on you go, onto your soapbox, louder and angrier, insulting more than the original provoker, and now you've lost ownership of yourself.

You now belong to the provoker, and if they are a narcissist, they're fulfilled. You've become their fighting pet. You hopped on their hamster wheel, and away you go. They got you and will keep on either painting the situation like they're a victim or the apparent victor in the scene. And you, you just exhausted all your valuable quality time on a person who didn't have your best interests at heart. Whether they can control themselves or not – *you can*. Once I noticed this I was like, whaaa? Hot damn, my emotions were mine!? They're MINE.

It's almost the same feeling that character Neo from *The Matrix* felt the moment he realized he knew Kung Fu. Hey, look at that. John Wick earlier, Neo now. Kind of a full circle! And both are Undercover Superheroes. I love how these things work themselves out. That's a Universe fist bump to the messages I'm hoping to get across to you.

In the remote-control theme, it reminds me of my early years as a mom, putting a children's show on for my daughter. The show was fine and almost over. I stepped away to wash some dishes and heard the spoiler music of a horror movie trailer. Because I didn't feel that was an appropriate thing to watch for my four-year-old, I ran to the table, grabbed the remote and hit stop (since this was a recorded show), and deleted it. There was no more use of it.

Our mind can do the same. Just stop what you're involved with and delete any future engagements, knowing it's of no more use to you. When we look at the provoker, they might feel negative, but I don't need to feel that way. They can throw ugly words toward me, but I don't have to catch it and keep it buried in my heart. I don't have to catch a thing.

Let the words

- fall on deaf ears
- go in one ear and out the other
- just tune out

Oh! Or you could just *change the channel.*

While I don't always understand the reason behind the ugly actions and words from people, I can at least take comfort in knowing about who I am. That I hold enough power to reclaim my own values. I can redefine broken and restrictive definitions and build a new foundation of my life.

As a child and toward my teen years, I felt like I was collectively placed in an emotional prison in some ghost town, but somewhere later in my young adult years, the keys were left hanging on a peg just outside my jail cell. All I needed to do was tie a few belts together to make a rope (yes, I'm a *Brady Bunch* fan) and put a valiant effort in to get myself out.

Once I did, I took notice that I went from a weakening stage to an awakening that ignited more powers within me. Powers that led me to my next missions.

Now, I know you've seen enough memes, read the articles and self-help books videos and presentations. There are so many resources externally flooding your eyes and ears. It's overwhelming. And, of all that's out there to choose, you decided to grab this book, and you've most likely read it to this point. If the purpose was only to hear my stories, I thank you for your time, and I hope they entertained you enough to share with you the world I was in, and you've now gotten to know me a little better.

But if you gained something more, something that hugged your spirit, or nodded along with some of the struggles you might still keep in the dark catacombs of your heart where no one has to see, I'm glad this book fell into your hands.

If no one ever speaks this to you, I ask that you hear my voice through the words, knowing that I'm speaking this to you, and for you, with a good love for your climb out from whatever trenches you're in and to step out into your inner light.

While the world's humans interact with you in ways to prick your finger, bruise you with their callous blows, and/or neglect the beat of your heart, do this: place both your hands on your heart and have a seat somewhere quiet that's for you and you alone. Stay still with your hands on your heart. Breathe normally and calmly. Focus your attention to your heartbeat.

The heart is the very first organ to develop when a baby is conceived. That means this beautiful heartbeat you're feeling has been with you since the beginning. When you look at your heartbeat, it reflects your life, literally and figuratively. I spoke of lessons and blessings earlier in this book – imagine blessings you receive as the peaks you see in the image provided, and lessons being the valleys. Even in between, the power of the pause is reflected. Yes, even your heart pauses for a moment.

Your whole life is shown in a heartbeat, and it stayed with you through it all, from the moment life began to where you are right now.

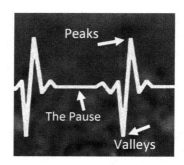

It's natural for most of us to want a life with no drama, pain, anger or conflict. But take a moment and think about what you're asking for – a life with no peaks or valleys. Just one long pause. Wouldn't that resemble a flatline? Funny that the words Rest in Peace connect us to death. Maybe the message there is that we really need to appreciate the ride and see this experience as an adventure filled with activities that bring us lessons and blessings for a fulfilling life? We all want to live in peace, but the trick is to live in order through the pattern our heartbeat provides.

I remember anytime my daughter fell, or spilled something, or tripped, anytime something appeared to be a big deal in her point of view, I'd rush to her, place my ear to her heart and take a deep excited breath saying, "oh! Hold on! Oh... oh there it is! Listen! Listen! Can you hear that? It's your heartbeat! You're doing just fine!" and I'd place her hand on her heart to feel her heartbeat. Why? Because I wanted her to know that nothing else mattered but her heartbeat.

Of course, we want everything in our body to work well, the distraction was designed to take her mind off of sweating the little things and tune into to the magnificence of her heart getting through that moment. If her heart can get through it, so could she. One day she bumped into the cabinet door, she was probably three, and instead of looking to me, or her chin quivering, or her eyes feeling sad, she put both hands on her heart to check it. She saw it was good and kept on keepin' on. Atta girl.

One of my favorite things to ask couples young and old is, "How did you meet?" and almost everyone I've asked has told me a love story that's had peaks, valleys and pauses. Love doesn't come to us through a flatline experience. Neither does making big-decision purchases (i.e. homes and cars, etc.). It happens to us through peaks, valleys, and pauses. There will be a time and place for the flatline, but our heart prefers to have you recognize its existence. By placing your hands to your heart you'll have a sweet and powerful reminder who's not only here with you but who reminds you how life actually works 24/7/365.

The heartbeat designed an adventure for you, and when you take on the experience with the powers and tools that you've been provided, you'll grow exponentially. You'll appreciate and value more. Your mind and body, in turn, will celebrate your life by flooding you with feelings of content, fulfillment, and confidence.

Chapter Eighteen: My Universe
Playlist: Just Like Fire – P!nk

Mission: Master your Universe

I guess I should finally introduce myself. I'm Anita Myers. Born and raised in Chicago and Chicagoland, Illinois. I'm a lover, a fighter, and a friend.

Of course, I could have told you the usual, professional resume-styled, thirty-second elevator pitch crap, but I don't want you to know me that way. I'm not the Homecoming Queen or the model, the dancer, the executive, the insurance broker, or even an online social media personality and co-host for a talk show called The Power Hour. I'm not the owner of a mind power training and development practice. I'm not someone's daughter, wife or mother, either. Those are all positions and missions I chose, held, am involved in, or are embarking on as added adventures within my existence.

They are all challenges and victories – experiences that pushed me to eventually reveal my powers. Who am I? It's going to sound a little out there to those of you who are incredibly grounded in being human. Yes, I'm human (whew). But everything I do comes from everything I am. There's energy existing within me, and within that energy exists powers – powers that I was born to use. My powers? It comes as a general trinity that drills down to a multitude of powers. My general trinity: I'm a lover, a fighter and a friend. Don't take those words so lightly.

I know you're looking for some magnificent action words resembling a *DC Comics* or *Marvel* level, but the truth is, what lives within me are ridiculously epic powers necessary to live passionately well in a world as we do, where selfishness, entitlement, and manipulation dwell and try to invade our values, relationships and the beauty life still has to unfold for us.

In the end, I believe that there's a fire needed to pave paths back toward being someone who loves well from the inside, and who pours quality love into others on the outside. Who embraces the word *friendship*, where gratitude, trust, and forgiveness play significant roles through the experience? Who fights with logic and respect for themselves as well as who they're speaking to, even when people aren't so respectful?

You have ridiculously epic powers, too – you just might not have been trained to identify and/or use them as often as I've used mine. You'll either naturally connect to or train in the powers you have once you recognize how to operate optimally within yourself.
Doing this allows me to extend the best of myself to people, situations, and challenges. I've learned to commit to the work that needs to be done, and to use my powers only for the greater good. And this

work – this dedication in building our ability to strengthen our powers into solid, productive habits is what eventually turned me into an Undercover Superhero.

I believe that everyone here is an Undercover Superhero, with powers waiting to be revealed to use for the greater good. You have powers that may have been covered up, eclipsed, or shadowed by family members, friends, society, or experience(s). Or maybe, you've noticed the powers you have, but struggle in breaking through to live a more powerful life filled with a considerable amount of quality and fulfillment in your day to day life.

You don't have to struggle anymore. The door is open. Just walk through and train in everything you already have. Harness all that incredible power in your mind. Gain control of it. Know what you're working with. The Universe within you and outside of you is stretching their necks, waiting to see your transformation.

I've learned to elevate my level of energy, to be strong enough to make decisions that work in my favor, so much that I wanted to bring what I did and still do to the foreground to help you and others reach greater pinnacles in life. Aren't you worth it?

(Answer: Yes! Survey says...100 points, you win!)

As my own story of life unfolded from a young age, I realized that asking for help wasn't worth the effort in the environment I was in; I'd either be criticized for asking, interrogated, told that those aren't questions to be asking, or neglected. If I voiced concern, it was considered silly, stupid, or not worthy enough to gain an answer. I saw disgust, head shakes, or neglect because they viewed me as a little kid who hadn't earned the rights to talk with them.

The climate of my early life created a separation of church and state between them as adults, and me as a kid, and while I want to understand the reasoning behind it, I didn't like the divide. Even if I believed I was useful, valuable and much bigger in maturity and appreciation to gain answers to many of my harmless curiosities – their negative attitudes and poor emotional self-control left me feeling small, undervalued and worthless.

My parents weren't monsters, and neither were the people who contributed their ugliness to the overall outcome, but their problems and decisions crafted an emotionally disengaged and abused life that taught me definitions that didn't equate to what a love story was supposed to feel like. And as much as I believe physical abuse is horrific, I think that emotional and psychological injuries create worse results.

Intangible harm is easy to hide and easy to give —
no proof for the predator to worry about. Everything
is just made up. Like it never happened. Can't really
hold it in court. No evidence. Yet.

If we could suddenly walk through a crowd and be
able to visually identify the stabs, lacerations,
broken structures within our emotional, intellectual
and spiritual "skeleton" in the people we pass by, or
talk to, we might gasp deeply seeing how many
more people we'd never imagine among us are
hiding decades of shattered structures within them,
smiling strong on the outside, broken and surviving
on the inside.

We might notice the strongest, happiest, funniest
person in the crowd barely holding it together on the
inside. We might see the horror in people we would
have never imagined living in such an annihilated
condition. We might come to understand better why
so many people prefer drugs, alcohol, crime, sexual
abuse, narcissism, gambling, smoking, eating, not
eating, emotional, unemotional and living in these
altered states, settling for experiences that increase
the risk of loss, and the neglect of gain.

I chose to stand back up and heal myself from the
damage I was living with. I know that collective
damage could have led me to my demise if I didn't
give myself that 0.5%. Once I decided to train hard,
living life with a more powerful lens – one that
offered grace, respect, compassion, and love *to

myself* - I became more than able and ready to share that bread of life to others who wander in their inner desert, accepting life as others made it for them.

I majored in marketing for my father, but I added a minor in psychology for myself, and later polished what I already learned on my own through my experiences and success rate through achieving a license and certification in life coaching and relationship coaching. I could take everything from my heart, mind, and spirit and pass that 0.5% baton and more to those who are ready to step into their light – into the Undercover Superhero world that awaits them.

There are more emotional deaths that take place from a slew of actions that can be healed. People metaphorically get consumed from the avalanches of life. They get thrown into a bad deal accidentally by being at the wrong place and time. They make decisions that hurt more than help. Eventually, they hit rock bottom, and there's no one to turn back the clock, swoop in and carry them out from that mindset.

The idea of being vulnerable is a new needed recognition for many who've been told in their past to suck it up, deal with it, quit crying, etc. They all reflect what I'll call the "piece de résistance," with the meaning being more of a resistance to attaining peace. All of those methods cajole human behavior to stifle feelings that need to be recognized.

I have honed in and mastered the process of observing, deconstructing and rebuilding new definitions that allow me to live with a win-win mentality – the kind of mental and emotional world where there are only two options to choose:

learn the lesson and believe in the blessing.

As an authority in the training of emotional mind power, my mission is for populations all over the world to heed my 0.5% through this book.

This fraction of a percent in effort spells possible. It's the beginning. It's the first step toward a powerful and quality life.

It is possible to climb out from sedentary, struggle, mundane, anger, confusion, loneliness, abuse and more – but the caveat is that this is an inside job.

Mission Possible is an inside job.
You have to get out of your own way.

- the way that was designed by other people's opinions that didn't match yours

- the idea that told you to settle because you didn't have the ability or knowledge to open the door to the better opportunity that awaits you

- the way that was created and became habitual, because you felt, or someone told you, that it was "the right thing to do."

- the way that someone controlled you to believe when you know you deserve so much better

- the way that someone steamrolled you to staying exactly where you are in the mundane and ordinary when, no matter what anyone says - if love becomes your engine - you are a treasure to be unearthed.

Listen, you are beyond extraordinary.

There is a one-in-400 billion chance for you to be created. You made it. There is a purpose for you, and while Life is your adventure loaded with action, challenges, lessons, and blessings, it offers so much love, encouragement, and support – you just have to do the proper training and prep to enter the better world that is on the other side of the unlocked door you're looking at.

Your mission, should you choose to accept it, is to harness your mind power so you can master your Universe.

As always, should you or any of your emotional powers disengage within the building process, your chances of immediate success will be slim pickings, and your extraordinary unlimited potential will self-destruct at the point of disengagement. This page will come to a close in five seconds.

Step into your light. Your power. Your existence. Recognize your personal power.

You do that, and you'll reveal the Undercover Superhero within you that's been on deck, waiting to conquer the world with you. ♥

About the Author

 Anita Myers, CPC, CRCS is a certified and licensed Life and Relationship Coach. She has a Bachelor's degree in Marketing and Psychology. None of those accolades and educational merits matter to her compared to the level of investment and passion in impacting, training, influencing, and networking for stronger, emotional wellness across the globe.

Anita's demonstration of mind power through her positive and productive strategies to spotlight the inner strengths of her clients and colleagues, earned her nickname/alias as "Anita Powers" from co-host Dolly Cortes of her social media talk show, *The Power Hour.*

She is the owner of InnerScope Consulting, a personal development training company, designed to provide training programs in life management, dating, relationships and parenting power, as well as the development of skills, breaking bad or unproductive habits and creating proactive and productive habits.

Through her LEAP training platform, she engages clients in her Life Enrichment and Application Programs, bringing personal purpose to the surface by way of a strong recognition of mind power: the energy behind the thoughts, feelings, and actions we are given to conduct our everyday lives.

Through Anita's guidance, knowledge, and training practices, she provides the perspective and strategies needed to disengage from poor, debilitating habits, responses, and actions, and transforms displaced energies into purposeful, power-packed experiences, that help to build a substantial, well-functioning, gorgeous mansion within the emotional landscape of the mind. Through the optimization of mind power, Anita aims to ignite generations to discover, train and master their Undercover Superhero qualities, talents, skills, challenges, and capabilities, so they can confidently master their Universe.

"It's an amazing feeling when you unlock gates to opportunities. You unleash desires you thought you couldn't have. You begin to feel stronger, more powerful and able to reach higher ground. It's quite superhero-esque, but aren't we? We just have to harness the vision and set ourselves free to reach that destination."

anita@innerscopeconsulting.com
InnerScope Consulting

The child

The teen

The young lady

The woman